D0516492

MODERN WORLD NATIONS

AFGHANISTAN	IRELAND
ARGENTINA	ISRAEL
AUSTRALIA	ITALY
AUSTRIA	JAMAICA
BAHRAIN	JAPAN
BERMUDA	KAZAKHSTAN
BOLIVIA	KENYA
BOSNIA AND HERZOGOVINA	KUWAIT
BRAZIL	MEXICO
CANADA	THE NETHERLANDS
CHILE	NEW ZEALAND
CHINA	NIGERIA
COSTA RICA	NORTH KOREA
CROATIA	NORWAY
CUBA	PAKISTAN
EGYPT	PERU
ENGLAND	THE PHILIPPINES
ETHIOPIA	RUSSIA
FRANCE	SAUDI ARABIA
REPUBLIC OF GEORGIA	SENEGAL
GERMANY	SCOTLAND
GHANA	SOUTH AFRICA
GUATEMALA	SOUTH KOREA
ICELAND	TAIWAN
INDIA	TURKEY
INDONESIA	UKRAINE
IRAN	UZBEKISTAN
IRAQ	

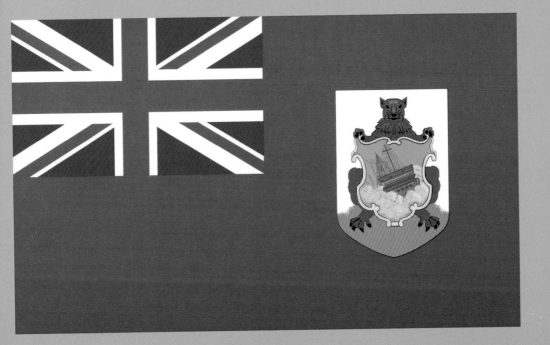

Bermuda

Richard A. Crooker
Kutztown University

Series Consulting Editor
Charles F. Gritzner
South Dakota State University

Chelsea House Publishers
Philadelphia

Frontispiece: Flag of Bermuda

Cover: These arches appear along the seacoast and form naturally when seawater weathers away the limestone rock from underneath.

CHELSEA HOUSE PUBLISHERS

EDITOR IN CHIEF Sally Cheney
DIRECTOR OF PRODUCTION Kim Shinners
CREATIVE MANAGER Takeshi Takahashi
MANUFACTURING MANAGER Diann Grasse

Staff for BERMUDA

EDITOR Lee Marcott
PRODUCTION ASSISTANT Noelle Nardone
PHOTO EDITOR Sarah Bloom
SERIES AND COVER DESIGNER Takeshi Takahashi
LAYOUT 21st Century Publishing and Communications, Inc.

©2002, Updated Edition 2005 by Chelsea House Publishers,
a subsidiary of Haights Cross Communications.
All rights reserved. Printed and bound in the United States of America.

www.chelseahouse.com

3 5 7 9 8 6 4 2

Library of Congress Cataloging-in-Publication Data

CIP Applied for 0-7910-8663-1

Table of Contents

Bermuda

Approaching Bermuda by air from the south side of the islands, one is struck by the varying shades of blue and green, from light turquoise to dark emerald, that characterize the land and sea.

Introducing Bermuda

B ermuda is a small group of islands in the western North Atlantic Ocean. It is about 650 miles (1,050 kilometers) from the United States. The islands are not associated geologically with the West Indies, which lie more than 800 miles (1,300 kilometers) to the south and southwest. Bermuda is a self-governing colony of the United Kingdom (consisting of England, Wales, Scotland, Northern Ireland, and outer islands). Complete with turquoise waters, clear skies, and a mild climate, it is an enchanting place to live. Bermuda's population is so small that an American professional football stadium could seat all of its inhabitants (63,500).

This book is one in a series of volumes about major world nations. Why is a book about a tiny cluster of isolated islands with a small population included in a series about major

Bermuda is a popular destination for novice snorkelers and scuba divers because they can walk off the beach into the water and see a wide variety of colorful sea life without needing a boat.

world nations? Bermuda is included because it is one of the wealthiest nations in the world. Described here is how geography and history converged to create the nation of Bermuda as well as an outline of its problems and future prospects.

Most of this colony's 400-year history is about economic survival rather than economic growth. In order to survive, Bermuda has taken advantage of its geographical situation between two economic powerhouses—Europe and North America. Only in recent decades has Bermuda become wealthy by successfully exploiting its location. The colony now provides financial services for international businesses. It also provides luxury facilities for hundreds of thousands of tourists from Europe and North America.

Geographical situation has probably played a more important role in Bermuda than in most countries. For example, would Bermuda have developed as it has, if it were situated in the middle of the South Atlantic Ocean? It probably would not have. St. Helena, another British island colony, has such a location. It is halfway between Africa and South America. It never developed a strong economy, because there has been little cross-ocean trade between these two continents. During the nineteenth century, its economy was limited to the provision of supplies for shipping and for the local garrison. Except for a small flax industry in the first half of the twentieth century, the island has had virtually no industry of its own. Nowadays St. Helena is largely dependent on aid from Great Britain.

Bermuda's development is only partly due to its situation between Europe and North America. Favorable location offers opportunities for people. People must take advantage of the opportunities. Bermudians did eventually take advantage of their location. However, they had to struggle with a limited natural resource base. Ultimately, they built a vibrant culture and nation.

Bermuda's culture is "very British" because it is a colony of the United Kingdom. However, Bermuda has always had closer economic ties to the United States than the United Kingdom. Bermuda's population is diverse racially and politically. However, its people work within its political system to solve national problems. The colony has had a long tradition of democratic self-government. That tradition has developed self-reliance, tolerance, ingenuity, and open-mindedness. Such qualities account for much of the success that Bermudians experience today.

Bermuda is a unique country. It has created its own style of architecture, dress, and way of life. Because of its strategic importance, Great Britain built many forts in Bermuda—so many that Bermuda became the "Gibraltar" (impenetrable stronghold) of the Atlantic Ocean. The colony has interesting contradictions. For example, Bermuda's towns have narrow, winding streets lined with seventeenth century buildings; yet these buildings have connections to the twenty-first century's World Wide Web. The islands are flooded with tourists but they have tiny coves for quiet escape. The hedge-rowed countryside is reminiscent of the Cotswold Hills of temperate England, but it also has palm trees from tropical Florida and the Bahamas.

Bermuda stands out among nations in other interesting ways. It sits on an ex-volcano. It has the world's northernmost coral reefs and mangrove swamps. Its reefs, lurking just beneath the ocean's surface, have sunk an untold number of ships, perhaps more than 500. No island in the Atlantic Ocean has a population density greater than that of Bermuda's. Bermuda is also the oldest colony of the British Commonwealth. Bermuda was the first island resort in the Atlantic Ocean. It was also the first island country to manage offshore banking accounts for international firms. Bermudians grew the first Bermuda onions (mild flat onion). They made the first Bermuda shorts (commonly called Bermudas). (Bermuda grass, however, did not originate in Bermuda; it comes from Eurasia and Australia.)

Bermuda is also the namesake of the infamous Bermuda

Due to Bermuda's strategic importance, Great Britain built many forts on the islands, including this one on Castle Island. In 1612 Castle Island was fortified by then-Governor Moore to protect Castle Harbour. These are the ruins that one can see today.

Triangle. This is a triangular area of the Atlantic Ocean. Bermuda is to the north, Florida to the west, and Puerto Rico to the south. Many ships and planes have disappeared in this area, and many people believe under mysterious

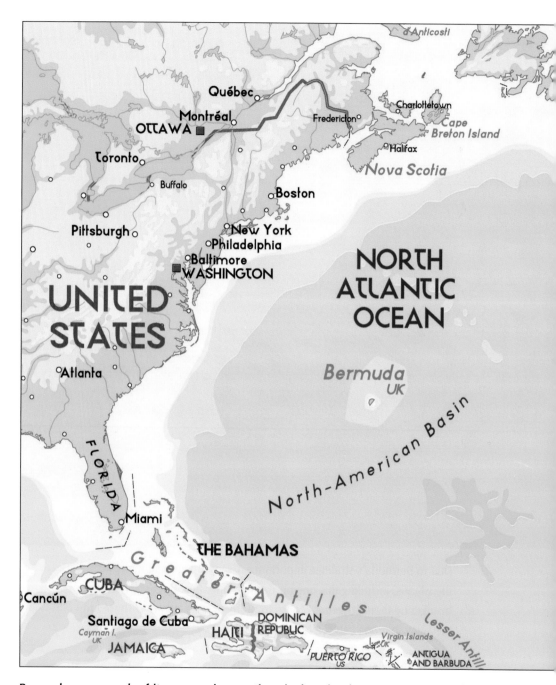

Bermuda owes much of its economic growth to its location between Europe and North America. It provides financial services to international companies and is a popular tourist destination.

circumstances. Fantastic theories explain these disappearances. They range from whirling vortexes of water to time warps and kidnappings by aliens. Human error and hurricanes are the more likely culprits. Bermuda's graveyard of reef-torn ship- wrecks might hold the bones of many of these missing vessels.

Horseshoe Bay is one of the most famous beaches on Bermuda due to its long, curved strip of pink sand. It is on the South Shore Road in Southampton Parish and despite its popularity, it can have treacherous undercurrents that make it dangerous for swimming and snorkeling.

2

Physical Landscapes

T he most obvious characteristic of Bermuda's physical landscape is its small size—nowhere can one get as far as a mile from the coast. Its land area is almost identical with that of Manhattan Island in New York. However, unlike Manhattan, Bermuda is not a single island. It is a small group of islands.

Bermuda is made of limestone. Coral reefs, turquoise lagoons, pink-tinted sand, and sea-carved cliffs fringe its coastline. Bermuda's rolling surface hides limestone caves. A mild climate and sweet-scented flowers blanket the rolling hills. Bermudians cherish their physical landscapes and speak of them proudly. Every year, American tourists flock to Bermuda in huge numbers to enjoy the physical charm of the islands.

The Islands

Bermuda is an archipelago (a group of islands) in the North Atlantic. It is 650 miles (1,050 kilometers) east of Charleston, South Carolina. It comprises about 138 small islands that together total just 22.7 square miles (58.8 square kilometers). People inhabit only about 20 of these islands. The archipelago is located 32 north latitude and 64 west longitude.

The seven primary islands form the shape of a fishhook. Starting at the north end are St. George's Island, St. David's Island, Grand Bermuda (or Main Island), Somerset Island, Boaz Island, Ireland Island South, and Ireland Island North. Together, the islands make up 95% of Bermuda's landmass. Bridges connect them, giving the impression that they are one long island.

The land surface consists of low rolling hills, reaching a maximum height of 259 feet (79 meters) at The Peak on Main Island. The main harbors are St. George's, Castle, and Hamilton.

Ex-Volcano with a Limestone Cap

The islands of Bermuda are exposed parts of a limestone cap that sits on an ex-oceanic volcano. Oceanic volcanoes form when magma (melted rock) erupts from beneath the sea floor and cools to form lava. More eruptions add more lava and the volcano grows toward the ocean surface. If there are enough eruptions, the volcano's summit reaches the surface and an island is born. In this manner, about 100 million years ago Bermuda's volcano became an island. Then, it stopped erupting. Geologists classify the volcano as extinct, meaning it will never erupt again.

The limestone cap of Bermuda formed on the volcano in the last 1.6 million years. The cap is made of ancient sand dunes that were hardened into rock. The sand grains were made of calcium carbonate (or lime) from skeletons of dead coral polyps (invertebrate animals). In ancient Bermuda, ocean waves broke up coral colonies growing on offshore reefs. The waves washed tiny grains of coral sand onto beaches of what was then a volcanic island. Winds blew the sand into huge piles, forming dunes on top of the ex-volcano.

Finally, glaciers melting and advancing on continents caused the level of the sea to move up and down many times, covering and uncovering the sand dunes. Each rise and fall took hundreds, sometimes thousands of years to occur. The wetting and drying of the dunes gradually cemented the sand grains together, forming the present limestone cap. This limestone is the preferred material for building houses in Bermuda because, unlike most types of massive rock, it is soft enough to cut with a wood saw.

The whole limestone summit is more than 200 square miles (518 square kilometers), nearly ten times larger than the total land area of the islands. This cap is like a giant saucer that is almost totally under the ocean. Its curved southern rim is above water and forms the islands. The remainder of the rim—to the north—forms a line of submarine (undersea) coral reefs called Rim Reef.

Ships going to Bermuda's harbors must first pass through Rim Reef. A reef is hazardous to sailors because it is a ridge of rock, lying near the surface of the sea, which may or may not be visible at low tide. Throughout Bermuda's history, an estimated 350 to more than 500 vessels have struck these reefs while making their approach to the islands.

Coral Reefs and Lagoons

Coral polyps are tiny animals that live together in colonies in warm, shallow seawater; when they die, their lime skeletons stay behind to build reefs made of limestone. An immense number of hard skeletons of coral polyps make up coral reefs.

Coral reefs surround Bermuda. There are two main reef areas. Rim Reef forms a broad arc stretching from the eastern side of St. George's Island to the southern end of Main Island. This reef is offset a great distance from the islands. "Barrier reef" is the name given to such a reef, because it is an obstacle to ships trying to reach land. There are three large lagoons (shallow water bodies) between Rim Reef and the islands. North Lagoon is the biggest, averaging about 5 miles (8 kilometers) across. Another lagoon is Great Sound, which lies between Somerset and Main islands. The third lagoon, Harrington Sound, is almost completely landlocked by Hamilton and Smith's parishes.

Rim Reef and the entire fishhook of islands keep out large waves of the ocean. Consequently, the lagoons have gentle currents and quiet waters. Coral and sea grass grow in abundance in such an environment. They are important parts of a lagoon ecosystem that supports many different types of animals, such as fish, crabs, sea urchins, snails, and clams.

The lagoon ecosystem has always been an important natural resource to Bermudians. Many of lagoon animals were important to the food supply of early settlers. Today, lagoons supply about one-fifth of the fish eaten by Bermudians, and their famous tranquil beauty attracts many tourists to the islands.

The second coral reef, the southern reef, is smaller. It forms a band of coral next to the southern shore of Main Island. The entire reef is not always submerged. Boilers, which are doughnut-shaped ridges of reef material, extend to the sea surface. Waves continuously break over and into the doughnut holes, making the water look as if it were boiling. "Fringing reef" is the name given to this type of reef because it is so close to shore.

Beaches and Limestone Sea Cliffs

Wind, rain, and surf have ground Bermuda coral, limestone, and seashells into talc-soft beach sand. Bermuda

The Bermuda Biological Station for Research hosts many groups that come to sample the pleasures of Bermuda. Yet, it is also an active research facility conducting a wide range of marine studies. These divers are visiting the station.

has about 26 miles of beaches. The sand is pink in color, especially in beaches along the southern shore of Main Island. Such beaches appear pink, as tiny red colored shells of dead, single-celled marine animals called forams (short for foraminifers) get mixed with other particles—broken clam and snail shells, sea urchin remains, pieces of coral—bleached white by the sun.

Bermuda's beaches do not form a continuous stretch of sand. The islands raise right out of the sea in many places, leaving no room for sand to accumulate. In such places, waves meet limestone head-on forming rocky sea cliffs (steep slopes that border the ocean). Wave energy has whittled these limestone cliffs into rugged, picturesque shapes. Beaches on the islands' protected northern shores tend to be small because waves and currents are too weak to supply large amounts of sand.

The most popular beach among tourists and probably the most photographed is Horseshoe Bay, which is on Main Island's southern shore in Southampton Parish. This beach is also a popular destination for islanders living in the nearby town of Hamilton. Another favorite of visitors is Elbow Beach on Main Island's northern shore in Paget Parish. The best beach for snorkeling is Tobacco Bay in St. George's Parish.

Limestone Hills and Soils and Disappearing Streams

Soft limestone is the only type of rock in Bermuda. This rock affects the nature of the land surface in four fundamental ways. First, the uniformity of rock means that small differences in elevation exist, making most hillside slopes very gentle. Second, the soil that develops from the soft limestone is not particularly fertile; it tends to be sandy or porous, so water, pulled by gravity, leaches (washes) a lot of soil nutrients (plant food) downward and beyond the reach of most plants.

Third, soft limestone is so porous that during storms rainwater does not even enter streams, but simply seeps into the ground. As a result, surface streams and freshwater ponds are rare. The streams have excess water in their channels for perhaps a few minutes. Ponds are small because they rely on rainwater, and extensive mudflats form around their edges during dry spells.

Fourth, the presence of soft limestone causes sinkholes to form at the base of some hill slopes. Sinkholes are saucer-shaped depressions found in limestone regions. They collect surface water, which then sinks and disappears as groundwater.

Limestone Cave Systems

In limestone regions such as Bermuda, acid water filters down from the sinkholes and dissolves (eats away) limestone to create an underground network of streams. These streams dissolve more limestone to form cave systems. Caverns are the largest caves. Sometimes roofs of caverns become fragile and collapse, leaving deep surface depressions with steep-sided slopes. When several caverns close to each other collapse, they create large depressions; only steep-sided, cone-shaped hills remain standing.

The caverns (or caves) of Bermuda formed thousands of years ago when sea level was lower. Today, most of these caves are underwater; the sea has partially submerged a few. Hamilton Sound is where the concentration of submerged caves is greatest. To the delight of scuba diving tourists and local islanders, several underwater caves here interconnect and form extensive cave systems with many colorful tropical fish and other sea dwellers.

The cool and quiet beauty of the islands' partially submerged caves draw thousands of visitors annually. The most famous semi-submerged cave system, Crystal Caves, is located at Bailey's Bay, north of Hamilton. In 1907, two boys, trying to find a cricket ball, accidentally found an entrance to the caves and crawled inside. These caves are an enormous underground network and one of Bermuda's most spectacular natural attractions.

The Crystal Caves at Bailey's Bay have attracted visitors for many years as evidenced by this vintage postcard. The formation took millions of years to create and there are a large number of large stalactites and stalagmites. These caves were discovered in 1907.

Climate

Perhaps the most striking characteristic of Bermuda's climate is its mild temperature. Its temperature prompted one observer in the early 1600s to remark "no cold ther is beyonde English

Aprill, nor heate much greater than a hott July in France."

Bermuda's temperatures are mild because of the Atlantic Ocean's influence. In summer, the ocean cools Bermuda by absorbing and storing a lot of the energy it receives from the sun rather than releasing it into the air. During Bermuda's warmest months, July to September, the average high temperature is a comfortable 84°F (29°C). In Bermuda's coolest months, December to March, the ocean warms the islands by releasing solar heat it stored during the summer. The resulting average low temperature is a pleasant 61°F (16°C).

Bermuda's winter temperatures are also mild because of the influence of the Gulf Stream. The Gulf Stream is a continuous current of warm tropical water. It flows north from the tropics and passes between North America and Bermuda. During the winter, the Gulf Stream warms cold air blowing from North America toward Bermuda. Because of the current's warming influence, no single year in Bermuda has ever had an average monthly temperature at or below freezing (32°F/0°C or less). The lowest average monthly temperature on record is 44°F (7°C), which occurred in February 1950.

Bermuda's mean annual rainfall is 55.5 inches (140.9 cm). The seasons distribute rainfall evenly throughout the year. Since the ocean surrounds the islands, the amount of water vapor in the air (humidity) is always high.

Tropical Storms and Hurricanes

Tropical storms and hurricanes occasionally add to Bermuda's rainfall totals. A tropical storm is weaker than a hurricane. Wind speeds for tropical storms are between 35 and 73 mph (56 and 118 km per hour). When wind speeds exceed 73 mph (118 km per hour), the tropical storm becomes a hurricane. Only about 10% of tropical storms grow to become hurricanes.

Most tropical storms and hurricanes originate south or southeast of Bermuda between 7° and 20° north latitudes. These storms usually travel west and miss Bermuda, which is located at 32° north. About every three years, an errant tropical storm or hurricane brushes or hits Bermuda directly.

Between 1870 and 2004, thirty-three hurricanes passed within 69 miles of Bermuda. Eleven of these tempests had direct hits on the islands. Interestingly, all the bull's-eyes took place in the months of August and September. One of the most powerful hurricanes struck on September 14, 1926, causing severe damage and several deaths. Despite the 1926 storm's importance, it has no name, as naming tropical storms and hurricanes did not begin until 1950. Probably the most damaging hurricane was Emily, which hit Bermuda on September 28, 1987. The storm packed wind gusts (but not sustained winds) to 125 mph (200 km per hour), injured about 200 people, but fortunately, it caused no deaths. The most recent direct hit was Hurricane Fabian on September 5, 2003. Fabian was the most powerful hurricane to strike the islands since Emily. The storm hit the islands with sustained wind speeds of 121 mph (195 km per hour). Four people died when fierce winds and towering waves swept cars on a narrow causeway into the raging sea.

Nature Preserves

Bermuda is densely populated and only small areas of natural habitat survive. Approximately 10% of the total land area of the country is forest or woodland. Owing to the moderating effect of the warm Gulf Stream, Bermuda is the most northerly site of mangrove swamp and coral reef formation.

The Bermuda Government has a system of laws to protect the remaining areas of natural habitat from development.

There are 12 nature reserves and 63 parks scattered throughout the islands. Some of the reserves include very small, uninhabited islands. Both reserves and parks are home to a variety of plants and animals.

Plants and Animals

Bermuda has no physical connection to a continental landmass. Therefore, wind, migratory birds, and ocean currents carried all life to the islands before the arrival of humans. Settlers who came to Bermuda also brought plants and animals to the islands, usually intentionally, sometimes accidentally.

Endemic plants and animals are those unique to an area: They do not exist any place else in the world. Endemics came early to Bermuda and lived on them long enough to gradually change and become very different from their ancestors. The most important endemic plants in Bermuda are the cedar tree and the palmetto, a small palm-like bush.

Endemic animals include the cuddly cahow (pronounced ka-how). This bird builds nests in the island's craggy sea cliffs. There are no endemic land mammals. The only land animal in Bermuda before human contact was the Bermuda skink, a rock lizard. Adult skinks are about 7 inches long. Shore cliffs are the skink's favorite habitat. The Bermuda skink is a reptile, as is a snake. However, there are no snakes, endemic or otherwise, in Bermuda.

Today, humans threaten most of Bermuda's endemic plants and animals with extinction. For example, the cedar tree and palmetto bush are nearly gone. Before people arrived, dense forests composed mainly of these two plants covered the islands down to the water's edge. Islanders cut down the cedar tree extensively, so that it almost became extinct in the seventeenth and eighteenth centuries. Houses, chests, and barrels were made of this fragrant wood. By the late 1940s, disease killed most of the few remaining cedar trees. The palmetto also suffered from overexploitation. Its fibrous leaves were useful in making thatch roofs and a variety of woven commercial products—from straw hats to ropes.

Only a few stubborn cedars and palmettos remain on the Bermuda islands today. In addition, early settlers killed the cahow in large numbers for food. Biologists declared the cahow extinct in Bermuda in the early twentieth century until they rediscovered it on small, isolated islands in Castle Harbour in the early 1950s. In recent decades, the number of cahows has risen slightly, because people have been protecting their breeding areas from more aggressive birds. Also critically endangered, the skink manages to survive best in remote sea cliffs on uninhabited islands.

Native plants and animals already inhabit a location when humans arrive, but they are not unique to the location. About 80% of the trees, plants, and shrubs in Bermuda came from the West Indies and southern Florida. The mangrove tree and bay grape are two noteworthy examples. Their seeds may have washed into Bermuda on the Gulf Stream from Florida or the Bahamas. Several additional native plants probably arrived the same way: the Spanish bayonet, purple-flowered morning glory, and prickly pear cactus are examples.

Among native animals, bats managed to fly from North America to these isolated islands. Bermuda's limestone caves are a natural habitat for these nocturnal, flying mammals. Many species of migrating birds call Bermuda home for part of the year at least. The majestic Tropic Bird or Longtail, named after its string-like tail, is one of the original natives that still breeds in the thousands each summer in rocky sea cliffs. A fierce competitor for breeding areas, it nearly wiped out the endemic cahow, a fellow sea cliff dweller. The Longtail's arrival each year announces the coming of spring.

The red-billed tropic bird is better known in Bermuda as the Bermuda Longtail. This migrating bird calls Bermuda home for only part of the year.

Native animals also make their home in the islands' shallow lagoons and reefs. Found there in abundance are colorful tropical fish, such as the queen angelfish, rainbow parrotfish, foureye butterfly fish, blue tang, triggerfish, and orange spotted filefish. The lagoons and reefs are also home to dozens of native coral species. These include brain coral, tree coral, sea fans, and sea rods. Other lagoon dwellers include brittle stars, sea horses, anemones, sea urchins, squids, conchs, slipper lobsters, and spiny lobsters.

The queen angelfish is just one of many colorful tropical fish that can be found around the reefs of Bermuda. The reefs form a relatively shallow platform that skirts the islands and allows light to penetrate below the water's surface.

Over-fishing of Bermuda's reefs has been a concern for some time. Almost exterminated by the 1980s were two popular food fish, the grouper and the snapper. In Bermuda, as in many West Indies countries, fishermen have used fish pots to catch reef fish. Fish pots trap any type of fish over a certain size. Since 1990, the government has regulated the number of fish pots, and the numbers of groupers and snappers have been rising as a result.

People introduce plants and animals to a location where they never existed before. Probably the most common introduced tree in Bermuda today is the casuarina, also known as the Australian or Whistling pine. After most of the cedars died in the late 1940s, this pine became the principal tree for making windbreaks on the islands. Other plant introductions are flowering evergreen shrubs (bushes), flowering plants, shade trees, and crops.

Early Bermudian settlers introduced flowering evergreen shrubs to grow tall hedges (6 to 20 feet) along roads. Hedgerow is the name given to rows of such bushes planted along either side of a road. Country roads in much of southern England had hedgerows and growing them in Bermuda was the settlers' effort to recreate that landscape. Today, during summer months in particular, vibrantly colored petals of oleanders, bougainvillea, hibiscus, pigeon berry, and poinsettia line the islands' narrow roads.

An English custom of growing flowers also led to the introduction of many garden ornamentals: multicolored patches of carefully tended roses, nasturtiums, geraniums, passionflowers, and birds-of-paradise are typically seen the yards of Bermudian homes.

Throughout Bermuda, flowering trees grow close to homes for shade. Such introductions include the avocado pear, mahogany tree, tamarind, pride of India, black ebony, and royal poinciana.

Early settlers had the idea of producing cash crops and brought many plants to the islands for this purpose. All such ventures failed because of poor soils and distance to markets. Now these same plants are shade trees or ornamentals, or they simply grow wild. The earliest settlers regarded the pomegranate tree as valuable for its fruit as well as for hedging. Settlers introduced several other cash-crop trees for their tasty fruits: the papaya (or paw paw), banana, calabash, mammee apple, and loquat. They also brought the castor oil plant to the islands to produce cooking oil. Another introduction, the tall, slender coconut palm is scattered around the island. It was not a successful crop, because Bermuda's temperatures are too cool for the fruit to develop properly.

Hogs were the first animals introduced by humans. People refer to hogs variously as swine, pigs, sows, or boars. No one is sure exactly who brought swine to the islands. Some historians say Spanish sailors on their way to the New World dropped them off as a food cache for their return trip to Spain. Other historians say that they were survivors of a shipwreck on Bermuda's reefs. Whatever their origins, the first hogs on Bermuda were immortalized on a copper coin used by early settlers. Called hog money, a hog's image appears on the coin. Today, a hog's image is on Bermuda's one-cent coin, called a *hog penny*. Wild hogs no longer exist in Bermuda.

The largest wild mammals in Bermuda today are rats. Their ancestors arrived as stowaways onboard a ship in 1614. They quickly spread throughout the islands, devouring crops on their way. By 1617, islanders were so concerned about the growing number of rats that they tried burning large sections of the cedar forest to get rid of them. Domesticated cats were introduced a short time later and successfully reduced their numbers. Rats are no longer a serious problem.

Bermudians imported an amphibian, a giant toad, in 1875 to control another introduced animal—cockroaches. People accidentally introduced cockroaches, which are notorious pests, many years before. The toad has a warty skin with brown or black markings and grows to about 6

The first hogs to reach Bermuda were later pictured on a copper coin that is known as the hog penny. The hog penny is a one-cent coin.

inches (15 centimeters) in length. The toad helped combat the resilient cockroach in earlier years, but modern-day pesticides are now in use and have proven more effective. However, toads have become a bit of a nuisance themselves, since they have few natural predators on the islands and their population has grown rapidly. Today, islanders call these toads "Bermuda road toads," because so many of them wander onto roads and into oncoming traffic.

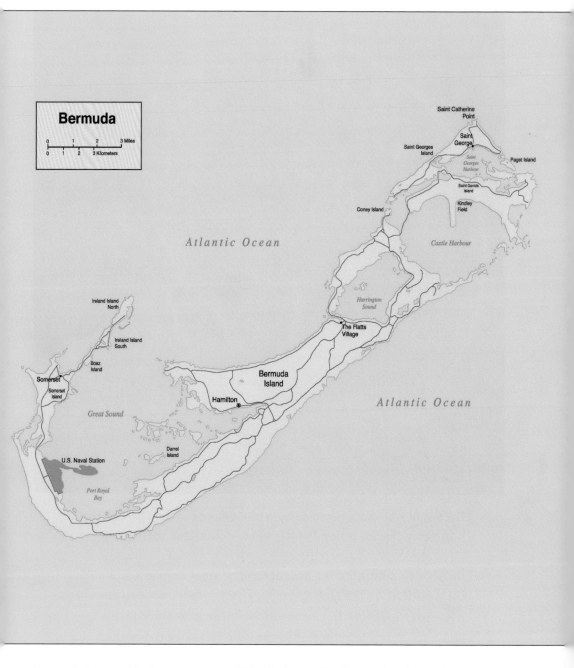

Bermuda is an archipelago, or group of islands, located in the North Atlantic about 650 miles off the coast of South Carolina. People live on only 20 of the 138 small islands that make up Bermuda.

Two additional amphibious introductions are whistling, nocturnal tree frogs. They are so small that they can sit on your thumbnail, hanging fast with tiny suction discs on long, slender toes. Their song, which is a loud bell-like chorus, is the sound of males trying to attract females. These musician wannabes keep a low profile until they feel like whistling, which is usually from April to November, when nighttime temperatures are 68°F (20°C) or higher. Some visitors say it disturbs their sleep, but others love it because it adds a unique sound to the night.

An interesting story about the "musical" talent of these whistling frogs involves John Lennon, musician and ex-Beatle. Lennon once rented a house in Bermuda, seeking quiet solitude so that he could write and compose songs. One evening he taped himself singing some of his songs unaware that he was singing to the accompaniment of one-inch whistling amphibians. Unfortunately for the frogs, who could have become world famous, the tape was just a trial tape.

Clipper ships were beautiful, swift vessels that plied the world's oceans carrying goods around the world. The *Comet*, shown here in a mid-nineteenth century illustration, had the misfortune to be caught in a hurricane off the coast of Bermuda.

3

Bermuda Through Time

The history of Bermuda is a story about how a small and isolated community has survived and triumphed. The story chronicles how Bermudians faced poverty, took advantage of opportunities, and eventually turned their islands into one of the world's most attractive tourist and banking centers. Of major importance was the island's unique geographical position, which on several occasions made Bermuda a place of economic and military importance in the North Atlantic region.

Discovery

The Gulf Stream assured Bermuda's early discovery. Homeward-bound European sailing ships used the north-flowing current to reach Europe from tropical America. It was only a matter of time before a nameless sailor sitting in a ship's crow's-nest would spot uninhabited islands on the blue horizon. The namesake of Bermuda is Juan de Bermúdez, a Spaniard who captained the first ship to see the islands around 1503. During the 1500s, sailors avoided Bermuda because of the dangerous reefs. Since hardly anyone would set foot on the islands to see what they were really like, seamen told fantastic stories about them.

By the mid-1500s, the islands were appearing on some maps with unflattering nicknames. For instance, Spanish maps referred to Bermuda as the *Islas Demonios* (Island of Demons). This was because as sailors passed by the islands, they were supposed to have heard shrill cries of demons (evil persons or spirits).

Navigational Landmark

Despite their bad reputation, Bermuda's reef-rimmed islands became an important navigational landmark during the sixteenth century. Ships bound for Europe followed the Gulf Stream north from the Gulf of Mexico, the West Indies, and Florida. When ship captains sighted Bermuda, they knew they had sailed far enough north to catch the prevailing westerly winds that would take them northeast toward Europe.

Sighting Bermuda and then resetting a safe course for home were reasons for celebration. Unfortunately, sailing ships sometimes approached Bermuda during storms. Fierce winds and pounding waves would prevent them from making accurate adjustments to their routes. As a result, many wayward ships crashed into the islands' unseen reefs and sank.

Islas Demonios No More

In 1603, strong winds forced a Spanish galleon into a reef. Captain Diego Ramirez and his crew set up camp on the north shore of the Great Sound and spent three weeks making repairs before returning to Seville, Spain. The survivors discovered that the straight trunks of the cedar trees, when cut lengthwise, made excellent planks for repairing their ship's damaged hull. They also found the sources of shrill, demon-like screams reported by the Spanish—wild hogs and cahows.

Ramirez's report of this adventure to the King of Spain provides the first written description of the islands' natural resources and a detailed map of Bermuda. However, Spain was not interested in colonizing small, remote islands.

Wreck of the *Sea Venture*

The wreck of the *Sea Venture* in 1609 is really when Bermuda history begins. It resulted in the first permanent human inhabitants of the islands and recognition by the British that the islands had useful resources.

In 1609, the English Admiral Sir George Somers, commanding a fleet of eight ships, set out from Plymouth, England, for Jamestown, Virginia. His ship was the *Sea Venture*. The admiral was employed by the Virginia Company of London (which had been given permission by England's King James I to colonize America). In those days, the English Crown often relied on companies owned by groups of influential merchants such as the Virginia Company to settle new lands.

Somers' fleet was to carry supplies and colonists to feed and reinforce the Virginia Company colony at Jamestown, Virginia. On the way, a fierce storm caught the *Sea Venture* and Somers lost contact with the rest of his fleet. The storm forced the *Sea Venture* to go off course and to crash onto a jagged coral reef three-quarters of a mile off the shore of Bermuda. Rowboats took everyone safely to shore, but the *Sea Venture* remained wedged atop the reef and was no longer seaworthy due to a severely damaged hull.

Somers promptly saw the value of the islands' natural resources and claimed them as an English possession. The survivors found that Bermuda's birds and fish, unaccustomed to humans seeking food, were tame enough that the castaways could catch them by hand. The castaways feasted on cahow, roast pig, turtle stew, and other island delicacies.

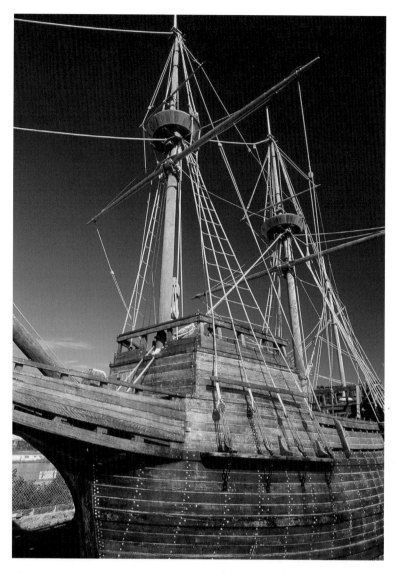

This is a replica of the *Sea Venture* that is docked on St. George's Island in Bermuda. When the *Sea Venture* wrecked in 1609 its crew came ashore and became the first permanent residents of the islands.

Under Admiral Somers' leadership, after 9½ months, the crew built two small ships, the *Deliverance* and the *Patience*. The castaways were finally able to continue their journey. In just two weeks, they crossed the deep blue waters of the

Gulf Stream to Jamestown. Two crewmen chose to remain in Bermuda to become its first permanent human inhabitants.

The *Deliverance* and *Patience* brought dried fish, fruit, and salted pork from Bermuda to the Jamestown colony. Six of the seven other ships in Somers' original fleet arrived nine months earlier with some food also. (The seventh ship was lost in the same storm that diverted the *Sea Venture.*) Nevertheless, Jamestown was still badly in need of more supplies, so Somers and members of his crew bravely volunteered to take the *Deliverance* back to Bermuda for more food to re-supply the colony. However, Somers fell ill and died not long after landing in Bermuda in 1610.

As was customary in those times, Somers' crew embalmed his body to preserve it for shipment back to England for burial there. As part of the embalming procedure, they removed and buried his heart and entrails (stomach, intestines, liver, and other organs). A small tomb in the town of St. George contains these remains today.

Bermudians are proud of the heroic story of the *Sea Venture* (1609–1610). Somers Day, the first Friday in August, is a national holiday in honor of Admiral Somers' fearless leadership. Somers is the Father of the Colony, for the wreck of the *Sea Venture* led to the deliberate colonization of Bermuda by the English. During the early period of the colony, the Virginia Company named the islands in his honor—Somers Islands. The *Sea Venture* is also honored in the colony's national seal: it shows the sailboat cast onto a reef and the nation's motto above, written in Latin, *Quo Fata Ferunt* (Wither the Fates Carry Us). Many Bermudians believe that like the castaways of the *Sea Venture*, a benevolent God cast them safely onto the shores of Bermuda.

Somers Islands Company (1615–1684)

When Somers' crew returned to England, the profit-seeking owners of the Virginia Company were very interested in the crew's description of Bermuda's food and timber resources. Company owners were also encouraged because Bermuda was uninhabited and therefore not open to Indian attacks as their Jamestown colony was. The owners decided that perhaps these islands could become a profitable colony in their own right.

In 1612, the Virginia Company sent to Bermuda a group of 60 English settlers, led by company-appointed Governor Richard Moore. Moore was an able carpenter and surveyor. He organized the building of St. George's, the first settlement of Bermuda, on St. George's Island. In 1615, with permission from the British Crown (the King of England), the owners of the Virginia Company formed a second company, the Somers Islands Company, to finance and manage colonization of Bermuda.

The Somers Islands Company sent many more settlers to the islands to ensure that it would make as much money as possible from cash crops. By 1615, the population had increased dramatically to 1,200, but most of the settlers were single men. The Company was concerned that unmarried men might leave the colony. Therefore, in 1621, the Company brought "certaine younge maydes" from England to the islands as prospective brides. Nevertheless, seeing yet another opportunity to make a profit, the Company required that if a single man wished to have one of these women as his bride, he would have to purchase her from the Company with 100 pounds of tobacco, an important cash crop and substitute for money at the time.

Despite the Somers Islands Company's successful efforts to settle the land, the land failed to yield its expected bounty. The soil was too shallow and the porous nature of the under-lying limestone prevented it from holding water. Efforts to grow sugarcane, the first cash crop, were disastrous. Next, the Somers Islands Company expected tobacco to be Bermuda's cash crop. The company grew and exported it to England for a short while, but Bermudian tobacco did not compete well against Virginia varieties. Other exports included potatoes, cabbages, and onions. However, the food supply shrank as the population of the colony grew. The Company abandoned the idea of cultivating such crops for export, but islanders continued to grow them for food instead.

Turks Islands Salt Works: Jobs for the Poor

By 1660, it became clear that agricultural exports were not going to assure the economic survival of the colony. In the late-1660s, the Company discovered that salt would provide a good profit. Salt was a valuable commodity before refrigeration, because it preserves food as well as seasons it. For example, salting beef, pork, and fish for storage was a common practice to prevent spoilage.

The Turks Islands, located nearly 1,200 miles (1,920 kilometers) to the south in the southeastern edge of the Bahama island chain, had shallow lagoons where workers could collect salt. The islands were uninhabited and unclaimed by any country, so the Company established a subcolony there from 1668 to 1801. Collecting and shipping salt would become the mainstay of Bermuda's economy for most of this period.

A major part of Bermuda's shipping was engaged in the Turks Islands salt trade. Company sailboats transported the salt to fishing ports in Newfoundland and Nova Scotia and exchanged it for salted codfish. The codfish became a staple food in Bermuda. Company vessels also took salted codfish to the West Indies to trade for sugar and rum. The Company then bartered rum and sugar for barrels of salt beef and salt pork in the American colonies, or for clothing and hardware in England.

Wrecking

Desperate islanders made extra money through the practice of "wrecking," or looting disabled ships that struck reefs surrounding Bermuda. Bermudians would not just wait for an accident to happen; they would rearrange beacons to confuse passing seamen and lure ships to the reefs. As soon as ships hit, the wreckers would dash out to loot them. Bermudians began "wrecking" hapless vessels in the 1670s and continued the practice until 1846, when the Governor of the colony had a lighthouse built to help ships avoid the most dangerous reefs.

Slavery (1616–1834)

Slavery is the owning or keeping of human beings. It is an economic institution. The cost of owning a slave is a very small amount, because an owner pays no wages to the slave. Therefore, the profit from practicing slavery is usually high. No matter what form it takes, slavery is immoral. Owners consider slaves as property, not human beings. Slavery deprives people of their most basic rights (life as human beings, liberty, and pursuit of happiness).

Settlers used slave labor in the New World to raise profits in their colonies. The colony of Bermuda was no different. The first slaves arrived in Bermuda around 1617, just after the Somers Islands Company was established. Most Bermudian slaves were black Africans. Slave ships brought them to Bermuda directly from Africa or took them first to sugarcane plantations in the West Indies. Slave owners there then re-sold to them to Bermuda slave owners.

Bermudian slaveholders dealt harshly with difficult slaves. Runaways received lashes at a whipping post. Punishment for plotting rebellions was even more brutal. Slave owners not only whipped plotters, but also branded an "R" for rebel on their foreheads. They also slit plot leaders' noses. Fortunately, such punishments seldom occurred in Bermuda.

Most Bermudian slaves were less inclined to run away or rebel because they had a better life than slaves did in other locations. Few Bermudian slaves toiled as unskilled laborers in fields, because landholdings were small. Owners gave most slaves highly skilled jobs, particularly in the maritime industry. Slave and slave owner were close socially because slaves usually lived in their owner's home. If the owner and his male slaves were mariners (seamen), they would spend even more time in close quarters onboard ships. Similarly, in Bermuda's small households, slave women and their white mistresses developed bonds of womanhood while their men were at sea.

The better conditions for slaves in Bermuda were still no excuse for treating people as property. Moreover, terrorizing slaves by threatening severe punishment is no less excusable than carrying out the punishment. The British parliament finally ended the practice of slavery in Bermuda in 1834.

Living From the Sea (1684–1865)

The Somers Islands Company treated the colonists poorly. Most islanders, whites and blacks, worked for very low wages in Bermuda or the Turks Islands. Under the rule of the Somers Island Company, islanders could also serve on company ships, but for very low wages as well. Bermudians could not participate directly in maritime (sea-faring) trade, because the Company would not let them build their own vessels.

Eventually, the colonists grew very dissatisfied; they took their case to London and sued the Company in court for "many misdemeanors and misgovernments by them committed." The court ruled in favor of Bermudians, and the British government took control of the colony in 1684.

The colonists, no longer bound by the Somers Islands Company's trade restrictions, were free to build their own vessels and to sail them wherever they pleased. They turned to the sea for economic survival and began to develop the independence and self-reliance that characterize them today. They became shipbuilders, smugglers, and privateers.

Shipbuilding

The wealthiest Bermudians invested money in building ocean-going sailboats and became sea-faring merchants. They employed many colonists as ship carpenters and as sailors. By the late 1790s, each year, Bermudians were building 40 to 50 sailing vessels, ranging in size from 40 to more than 200 tons. They sold about two-thirds of the vessels abroad.

By 1790, Bermuda's sailing vessels were "some of the fastest sailers [sic] that ever crossed the ocean." A French visitor, M. Jean Crevecour, said, "their ships are preferred above all others for navigation and smuggling in the West Indies." Bermudian vessels, often owned and manned by Bermudians, were among the main carriers of goods between ports stretching from Newfoundland to Barbados.

Smuggling

A smuggler brings goods secretly into or out of a country, usually to avoid paying taxes on the goods. In Bermuda, before going to the islands' official port of entry, where taxes on all imported goods were paid, vessels would quietly slip into one of many secluded inlets (entrances to small bays) to unload their illegal cargoes.

Goods were also smuggled out of Bermuda. Small-scale export smuggling was widespread. However, an exceptionally important incident of export smuggling occurred when several Bermudians conspired to smuggle British gunpowder to American rebels at the beginning of American Revolution in 1775. This was an unpatriotic act by the islanders, since Bermuda was a British colony and the Americans were fighting the British. However, food was in short supply on the islands, so the colonists agreed to smuggle out the gunpowder if the Americans would give them a one-year supply of food. In August 1775, Bermudians broke into the British arsenal in St. George, where the gunpowder was stored, loaded it into rowboats, and took it to waiting American rebel ships. Bermuda received food shipments as payment, but the islanders remained loyal to Great Britain during the remainder of the war.

The entire colony paid dearly for the role of Bermudian smugglers in the War of 1812. This war pitted Great Britain against the United States and lasted from 1812 to 1814. In August 1814, Bermuda was the launching point of the British Navy's successful attack on Washington, DC. The attack resulted in the White House and much of Washington, DC, burning to the ground. In response, the American government ordered all United States ships to confiscate the cargo of any ship flying the British flag. As a result, American warships captured or destroyed most of Bermuda's merchant fleet. The Bermudian economy, which depended heavily on trade, was devastated.

Privateering

A privateer is a "hired gun." A country hires him to sink, harass, or capture enemy ships in times of war. A privateer is different from a pirate, because a pirate does not work for a country to aid it in war. Pirates are lawless murderers, out to attack any rich prize no matter what country they are attacking. Only two Bermudians became famous pirates, John Bowen and Nathaniel North. Neither Bowen nor North used Bermuda as a base, however. Although they plied the oceans together for a while, Bowen's headquarters was on the Indian Ocean island of Mauritius and North's in Madagascar, which is also in the Indian Ocean.

Bermudian privateers worked primarily for the British, who fought wars against Spain, France, Holland (the Netherlands), the American colonies, and, later, the United States. Privateers were paid large amounts money for their "booty," which might include captured ships and crews as well as cargo. However, being a privateer was dangerous, since the

This photograph was taken in 1862 and shows the *Bermuda*, a blockade runner during the Civil War. Bermudan's sympathetic to the South used such ships to get supplies through to Confederate troops and their supporters.

enemy would sometimes capture or destroy even swift Bermudian vessels.

Naval blockades use warships to prevent passage in and out of enemy ports in time of war. The American Civil War (1861–1865) saw northern Federal States fighting southern Confederate States, which wanted to breakaway from the Union. When this war began, the Federal States used its warships to blockade southern ports. The British Queen declared England's neutrality in the war and prohibited British subjects from taking part in it.

The Federal blockade was set up to prevent supplies from

reaching Confederate troops and their supporters. However, "neutral" Bermudians were sympathetic to the South (because they, too, had been slave owners) and became middlemen in maritime smuggling between Britain and the Confederacy. St. George was the launching point for the blockade runners. British vessels brought gunpowder, munitions, and food to the town. Loaded with these goods, confederate paddle wheelers driven by steam and sail, slipped through the North's blockade. So did Bermuda's fast cedar-built sloops.

Confederate and Bermudian vessels took southern cotton back to Bermuda on their return trips. From there, British vessels smuggled the cotton to England's textile mills. Successfully running the blockade brought immense profits to Bermudian middlemen, officers, and crews.

The town of St. George especially benefited from the Federal blockade. At the outbreak of the war, stores and taverns seemed to appear overnight to serve seamen carrying pockets full of money. However, the boom ended just as quickly when the Confederates surrendered and the United States shut down the blockade. Bermuda's shipping industry, reliant as it was on smuggling, all but collapsed after the war.

Winter Vegetables (1870–1930)

During the late 1800s, the age of "steam" began to replace the age of "sail." New ocean-going steamboats were starting to carry more cargo and deliver it faster than sailboats. The United States and British steamboat companies took control of the Atlantic trade. Bermudians responded by making a great occupational change from the sea to the land.

Throughout the 1870s and 1880s, islanders turned to the soil and gradually developed a specialization in production of vegetables—onions, celery, potatoes, and tomatoes. Bermuda grew these vegetables for the winter market in New York City. American steamboats (steamers) delivered them fresh to produce markets there.

Bermuda's onions became so famous that the island group was widely referred to as The Onion Patch during this period. In addition, the Easter lily, introduced from Asia became extensively cultivated for exportation of bulbs and buds to the United Kingdom, the United States, and Canada.

Despite the renewed emphasis on agriculture, Bermudians were not particularly good farmers. Consequently, until the mid-1920s they occasionally brought indentured farm workers to the islands. (Indentured workers are laborers who sign a contract in which they agree to perform work for a certain length of time.) Bermuda brought most of the workers from the Portuguese islands of Madeira and the Azores. Thrift, skill, hard work, and good manners became the trademark of Portuguese workers. Bermuda invited many of them to remain on the islands after their indentured service was completed.

In 1930, Bermuda's specialization in winter vegetables came to an abrupt end when the United States passed the Smoot-Hawley Tariff Act. This act raised substantially taxes on food imports. As a result, prices of Bermudian vegetables sold in the United States skyrocketed to levels higher than Americans could afford.

Bermuda's small size would have doomed agriculture anyway, with or without the Smoot-Hawley Tariff Act. This tiny colony would not have been able to compete against giants like California, Texas, and Florida. These states began shipping huge amounts of winter vegetables to cities in northeastern United States after the Second World War.

Agriculture barely exists in Bermuda today. Texas now grows most of the Bermuda onions. Bermudian farmers tend to small garden plots to supply fresh vegetables to islanders and tourists. There are a few small dairies also. However, the islands still export the Easter lily, because a long history of marketing has made it a household word in the United States. Even so, most of the Easter lilies that Americans purchase today are grown in the United States.

The Princess Hotel opened in 1884 and became the first island resort hotel in the Atlantic Ocean.

Rise of Tourism

Bermuda was the first island resort in the Atlantic Ocean. The earliest tourists who came to the islands were from New York City. They boarded steamers that were on their return trip to Bermuda, after having delivered winter vegetables to the New York market. Tourists came as a mere trickle at first and stayed for just the winter months. Princess Louise, daughter of Queen Victoria and the wife of the Governor General of Canada, put Bermuda on the map for North American tourists. She paid a long visit to Bermuda in 1883.

Newspapers reported Princess Louise's stay in Bermuda. Then, with much fanfare, Bermuda opened its first seaside resort, The Princess Hotel (named after Princess Louise), in Hamilton in 1884. Next, journalists visited the islands, including American travelers such as Mark Twain who wrote several flattering articles about Bermuda in *Harpers Magazine*.

By the early twentieth century, Bermuda had become a trendy winter destination for wealthy visitors. After luxury steamship liners began arriving in the 1920s, the islands' tourist industry moved ahead of agriculture. Airline passenger flights to Bermuda started arriving in 1937. After the Second World War ended, the United States opened American-built Kindley Air Force Base to civilian traffic, giving tourists from the United States' east coast easy access to Bermuda.

In the 1960s, airline technology moved from propeller to jet engines. As a result, Bermuda suddenly became accessible to tourists in just a few hours, making weekend visits possible. By the 1980s, Bermuda reached its peak as a popular destination for tourists.

Second World War (1939–1945)

During the Second World War, authorities strictly rationed food and other necessities. Also, the government forbade travel out of the islands, and streets were in total darkness at night. The war brought tourism to a halt. However, Bermuda's tourist hotels earned money for the islands. Thousands of British and United States personnel were housed in them; their governments paid for their food and lodging. British intelligence agents (code breakers) took over the Princess and Bermudian hotels, the islands' two largest hotels. Their job was to uncover messages sent by enemy spies between the United States and Europe. A number of spies were unmasked.

Bermuda also served as a port for Britain's Royal Navy, which sought out German battleships and submarines that threatened allied shipping lanes in the North Atlantic. United States personnel were in Bermuda to build and operate Kindley Air Force Base on St. David's Island. Land reclaimed from Castle Harbour made up most of the base; so building it actually increased Bermuda's total landmass by 5% by adding another 1.25 square miles.

Bermuda's wartime economy did not suffer too much, since large numbers of American and British soldiers stationed in Bermuda had money to spend. Bermudians were probably wealthier after the war than before it started.

Population Growth (1945–Present)

The most important change in Bermuda since the Second World War has been its growth in population—it more than doubled in size from about 31,500 people in 1945 to 63,500 in 2001. Population density (the average number of people per square or per square kilometer) on the islands increased as the total population grew. Open areas in the countryside between villages filled with suburbs. (Suburbs are small communities whose inhabitants work and shop elsewhere.) By the 1970s, land for building separate homes was so scarce and expensive that Bermudians began purchasing condominiums (owner-occupied apartments) rather than homes. Nature reserves, parks, golf courses, and privately owned estates accounted for the few remaining open spaces on the islands.

Tourism spurred most of Bermuda's post-war population growth. It created jobs in building construction. The newly built hotels, restaurants, and department stores offered many service type jobs—managers, waiters, clerks, salespersons, and accountants. Black immigrants from the West Indies came to the islands to take most of these post-war jobs. Eventually, as discussed in Chapter 6, Bermuda would become a successful center for international business as well as tourism.

Fort Hamilton is a massive fortification that overlooks Hamilton and its harbor. At noon on some summer days the Kilted Bermuda Isles Pipe Band performs along with drummers and dancers.

4

People and Culture

ark Twain, author of *The Adventures of Tom Sawyer* and other famous books, spent his twilight years visiting Bermuda and getting to know its people. He once wrote jokingly that Bermudians are "people on their way to heaven who stopped at Bermuda and thought they had arrived." Twain's observation that Bermudians think they live in heaven is untrue, of course. However, if it were true, it would explain why these islanders have come from so many different places. Bermudians are a population built from African blacks, West Indian blacks, the British, Americans, Canadians, Portuguese, and American Indians. The settlement patterns, pastimes, and customs that these people share are threads that weave their lives together.

Population

Bermuda's population is 58% black, 36% white, and 6% other. Nearly 80% of Bermudians were born on the islands. Among islanders who were born elsewhere, about 30% were born in the United Kingdom, 20% in the United States, 13% in the Azores Islands or Portugal, 10% in the British West Indies, and 10% in Canada.

The black majority population has two slightly different groups: Bermudian blacks and West Indian blacks. Both groups have African ancestors. Slave traders purchased slaves, with rum and trinkets, from local African tribes who "tore them from their families." Bermudian blacks came to Bermuda first. They came as slaves from two regions, West Africa and the West Indies. After the British abolished slavery in 1834, most stayed in Bermuda and adopted the British culture as their own.

West Indians, the second group of blacks, came later. They began emigrating from the West Indies to Bermuda as free people in the 1880s and 1890s. They came from St. Kitts, Nevis, Antigua, and other small, mainly British, islands. By the time they began coming to Bermuda, West Indian blacks had developed customs, beliefs, and accents of speech slightly different from Bermudian blacks. Since their arrival in Bermuda, many West Indian blacks have kept these differences, because they have maintained close contacts with relatives living in the West Indies.

Most Bermudian whites are descendants of early British settlers and British immigrants. Some of Bermuda's families trace their roots to original British settlers of the islands. There are also whites of Portuguese descent. Their ancestors were poor farmers who went to Bermuda from two Portuguese islands, Madeira and Azores, beginning in the middle of the nineteenth century (see Chapter 3). Bermudian Portuguese own most of the remaining farmland on the islands. Others live and work in the town of Hamilton. White Canadians and Americans or their descendents are also citizens of Bermuda. Many of these North Americans, as well as people from the United Kingdom, mainland Europe, and the British West Indies, originally came to Bermuda on business trips or as tourists, but have since returned to become citizens of Bermuda.

Because of the physical and personal closeness of the white and black races in Bermuda, many Bermudians are actually mulattos, people whose families include both white and black ancestors. Bermudians refer to blacks or mulattos, regardless of darkness of skin color, social position, or geographic origin, as "coloured Bermudians." There is no social stigma attached to the name.

Descendents of American Indians also live in Bermuda. They live mainly on St. David's Island. Their ancestors were mostly Mahicans who lived as slaves in what is now New York State. Their owners sold them to slaveholders in Bermuda. After the British freed all its slaves, the Mahicans played a prominent role in Bermuda's maritime trade. They became members of boat pilot crews and were good at their work. A boat pilot crew's job was to take a small rowboat out to sea to meet a ship seeking safe passage to St. George's Harbour. Once contact with a ship was made, a member of the boat pilot crew would board it and help guide or "pilot" it through Bermuda's treacherous reefs and into the harbor. The rest of the crew would row back to St. David's Island. This was no easy task, as the crew usually rowed more than 20 miles out to sea to meet the ship. Only a few Mahican descendants live in Bermuda today, but their presence adds to the diversity of people living there.

Bermudians take great pride in their diversity and their ability to live together. The human fabric of their society is

A Bermudian girl in front of the Ethiopian Orthodox Church in St. George's, one of a number of churches of varying denominations in Bermuda.

Atlantic Ocean Island Countries	Population Density—Persons per mi^2 (Persons per km^2)
Bermuda	2,291 (1,154)
Jersey	2,021 (780)
Barbados	1,672 (646)
Puerto Rico	1,109 (428)
Martinique	1,011 (390)
Aruba	956 (369)
U.S. Virgin Islands	800 (309)

Table 1: Highest Population Densities of Island Countries in the Atlantic Ocean

strong. Bermuda's constitution reflects the value of human diversity, as it is written to protect the rights of all its citizens to act, speak, work, play, and worship as they wish.

Population Density

Population density is the number of persons per square mile or square kilometer. Bermuda's population density is higher than that of any other island country in the Atlantic Ocean, including countries in the Caribbean Sea. The colony's density is 2,991 persons per square mile (1,154 per square kilometer). The island country of Jersey, located near the English Channel, has the second highest population density— 2,021 persons per square mile (780 per square kilometer). See Table 1 for additional comparisons.

Main Island is home to 80% of Bermuda's population (Table 2). Pembroke Parish (population 10,600) has the highest population density, 5,048 persons per square mile

PARISHES AND CITIES (LISTED ALPHBETICALLY)	POPULATION 2004	AREA SIZE	POPULATION DENSITY (PERSONS PER MI²/KM²)
Devonshire	7,500	1.9 mi² (4.9 km²)	3,947 (1,531)
Hamilton (City)	1,000	0.3 mi² (0.7 km²)	3,333 (1,429)
Hamilton	5,400	2.0 mi² (5.1 km²)	2,700 (1,059)
Paget	5,200	2.0 mi² (5.3 km²)	2,600 (981)
Pembroke	10,600	2.1 mi² (5.4 km²)	5,048 (1,963)
Saint George (City)	1,800	0.5 mi² (1.4 km²)	3,600 (1,286)
Saint George's	3,800	3.6 mi² (9.3 km²)	1,056 (409)
Sandys	7,500	2.6 mi² (6.7 km²)	2,885 (1,119)
Smiths	5,800	1.9 mi² (4.9 km²)	3,053 (1,184)
Southhampton	6,300	2.2 mi² (5.8 km²)	2,864 (1,086)
Warwick	8,800	2.2 mi² (5.7 km²)	4,000 (1,544)
Total	**63,700**	**21.3 mi² (55.2 km²)**	**2,991 (1,154 km²)**

Table 2: Population, Area, and Population Density by Parish

(1,963 persons per square kilometer), which is more than twice the national average. Saint George's Parish, which includes St. George's and St. David's islands, has the lowest population density; 1,056 persons per square mile (409 persons per square kilometer). The presence of the Bermuda International Airport, which makes up about one-fourth of the Parish's land area, is the reason for St. George's low density.

Settlement Patterns

Despite Bermuda's dense population, homes on the islands align along main roads rather than build up in high-rise apartments. As far as the casual visitor can tell, Bermuda does not seem to be crowded with people at all. This is because homes hide behind well-trimmed hedgerows that line the islands' roads. In reality, there is very little land available for more homes. Parks, nature preserves, land for recreation (such as golf courses), and small garden plots take up almost all the open space that remains.

There are only two municipalities in Bermuda. (Municipalities are towns or cities that have their own elected officials, such as mayors and councils.) Hamilton, the capital, is Bermuda's second largest city (population 1,000). It is located in Pembroke Parish and has a delightful view of Hamilton Harbour. In 1815, Hamilton, which is in the center of the islands, replaced St. George (the colony's original capital) because of its ease of access. As the seat of government and the center of offshore banking, Hamilton is a busy town. Because of its importance, it is a transportation hub, a major marketplace, and the location of most businesses in Bermuda. The focus of activity is Front Street, which is a harbor front road lined with well-kept Victorian buildings.

Hamilton is crowded during the workweek because many people who have jobs there commute into town from surrounding Pembroke Parish. Although it is not Bermuda's largest municipality, islanders usually refer to Hamilton as "the town," because it has great importance to the country's economy and national life.

Bermuda's second municipality, St. George, is the island's largest city (population 1,800). The town is on the southern shore of St. George's island and overlooks the glimmering waters of St. George's Harbour. Founded in 1612, St. George was the first settlement and capital of

Hamilton is the capital of Bermuda and it is the business and governmental center of the islands. Front Street is a commercial center and many people visiting from the cruise ships come into town to eat, drink, and buy a variety of goods.

Bermuda. Like the town of Hamilton, it has a dense population. Unlike Hamilton, most of the people who work in St. George also live there. Fewer commuters are hurrying to work, so life in the town seems to have a slower pace.

Although St. George lost its role as capital in 1815, it is an important tourist attraction. Much of the town's charm comes from its historical architecture. As the original seat of government and oldest town, St. George is where the colonists developed a style of architecture best suited to the local climate, local building materials, and living requirements. This architecture is common throughout the island, but many of the best and earliest examples are in St. George. The town's original alleyways remain intact. Most of the colonial era buildings that line the alleyways that were once homes are now museums, public meeting places, churches, and shops.

The settlement pattern outside of Hamilton and St. George is mostly of the "string-village" type, since neighborhoods form narrow ribbons along main roads. There are a few small agglomerated settlements. These are settlements that spread from centers rather than along roads. Two such centers are large enough to be called villages—Flatts Village (in Smith's Parish) and Somerset Village (in Sandys Parish). Before the twentieth century, Flatts Village was a smuggler's haven. A small island just offshore from the village is where islanders executed people accused of witchcraft in the seventeenth century. Today, this village has a dozen or so businesses and one of Bermuda's principal attractions—the Bermuda Aquarium, Museum and Zoo.

Somerset Village has no major attractions, so visitors tend to overlook its quiet charm. Its namesake and founder of the colony, Sir George Somers, enjoyed the view from the site where the village was eventually located. At the north end of the village is the famous Somerset drawbridge. The bridge joins Main Island to Sandys Island. It is the smallest drawbridge in the world, because when it lifts, it opens up just a 30-inch span, which is enough to let through the mast of a sailboat.

Tucker's Town appears as a place name on maps of Bermuda, but unlike Flatts and Somerset villages, it is not an agglomerated settlement. Tucker's Town is actually the name of a broad area of fashionable development; it includes a scattering of millionaire estates and the exclusive Mid-Ocean Club. The Club has been in existence since the early 1920s. It was the first large tourist development in the islands and became a popular destination for Americans. Many famous people have played on the Club's golf course, including Sir Winston Churchill (a former Prime Minster of Great Britain), United States Presidents Dwight D. Eisenhower and George Bush Sr., Babe Ruth (the baseball player), and Sam Snead (the golfer).

Most other settlement agglomerations in Bermuda are large luxury hotels for tourists or small cottage colonies owned by wealthy people, primarily foreigners. Both hotels and colonies are set off from main roads, and most of them have access to private beaches and golf courses.

British Influence

Since Bermuda is a colony of the United Kingdom, many customs of daily life give the islands a British flavor. For example, everyone speaks English, people drive on the left-hand side of the road, judges and politicians wear white wigs, police are called bobbies, tea is a favorite afternoon drink, the birthday of the Queen of England is a national holiday, and cricket, which is a British game, is Bermuda's most popular sport. Bermudians observe several other British holidays in addition to the Queen of England's birthday. Islanders celebrate such occasions with full British pomp and splendor, including playing music with Scottish bagpipes (Scotland is part of the United

This drawbridge at Somerset is the smallest drawbridge in the world. Its 30-inch opening allows only the mast of a sailboat to pass through.

Kingdom), flying the Union Jack (the flag of the United Kingdom) and singing "God Save the Queen."

There are additional British influences. Islanders have named their towns and roads after the colony's early

British settlers. They also use British rather than American English spelling. For instance, the British spelling of the word "color" is "colour" and the word "harbor" is "harbour." Bermudians also use the British way of writing dates. They write the day of the month first, then the month and year: 18 December 2005 or 18-12-05. The United States way is to write the month first, then the day and year: December 18, 2005, or 12-18-05. Islanders also prefer the English system of weights and measures over the metric system. For example, they use pounds rather than kilograms to measure weights, and feet rather than meters to measure distances.

The British influence is so strong that islanders speak with a British accent. However, Bermuda's spoken English is not a clone—a perfect copy—of "The King's English." The islands' great geographical distance from Britain and its cultural diversity have developed unique pronunciations and expressions. For example, "w" is often pronounced "v," so that "welcome" sounds like "velcome." And -ing sometimes sounds like -in, so that "wedding" sounds like "weddin." Some common expressions are "de oda" for "the other," "byes and gals" for "boys and girls," "ace-boy" for "good friend," "wangin" for "driving really fast," and "horse" for moped or motorcycle.

Formal settings require the King's English. However, on the street one can hear informal speech laced heavily with the islands' local dialect. For example, a casual conversation might include a sentence such as the following: "De oda day my ace-boy went wangin down de road on a horse."

Black Influence

Blacks work and play side by side with whites as laborers, sales clerks, teachers, lawyers, doctors, and teammates. However, the stamp of black culture on Bermudian daily life is not obvious. Its greatest impact comes on certain holidays when black men and boys do a dance called Gombey (pronounced gum-bay). Gombey is unique to Bermuda. It has roots in West African tribal music but incorporates influences from Christian missionaries, the British military, and American Indians. The musical rhythms and acrobatic movements are from African dance. The dancers act out stories based on the Bible. The military influence appears in the use of a fife (usually a soda bottle), as well as whistles, drums, and cracking whips. The American Indian influence is evident in the dancers' colorful costumes that include tall headdresses and bows and arrows.

Gombey dates from the mid-eighteenth century, when costumed African slaves celebrated Christmas by singing and marching through the streets. Black Bermudians now perform it throughout Bermuda on December 26, which is Boxing Day (a national holiday of giving to the less fortunate), and New Year's Day. Other African-related influences come by way of the West Indies, such as the popularity of reggae, steel drum, and calypso music.

Religion

Most islanders are Christian. The Anglican Church (The Church of England) is the largest Christian denomination. There are also Christian worshippers of the Roman Catholic, African Methodist Episcopal, Methodist, and Seventh Day Adventist faiths. A small number of Bermudians are Baptist, Presbyterian, Christian Scientists, Jews, Jehovah's Witnesses, Ethiopian Orthodox, and Muslims.

Visitors to Bermuda notice right away the many churches that are scattered throughout the islands. Indeed, Bermudians say that the colony has more churches per square mile than any other country. Churches are some of the islands' oldest structures. For example, St. Peter's Church, which is in the center of town of St. George, is the

The Cathedral of the Most Holy Trinity, or the Bermuda Cathedral, is the mother church for the Anglican (Church of England) diocese in Bermuda.

oldest continually used Anglican church in the Western Hemisphere. Churches are also Bermuda's most impressive buildings. For instance, the Cathedral of the Most Holy Trinity in Hamilton is the tallest building in Bermuda. The large number of churches exists on the islands because most Bermudans have a spiritual nature. The ability of every man, woman, and child to worship freely in their house of worship is a great testament to Bermuda's democratic tradition.

The Honorable Albert Jackson, president of the Bermuda Senate in 1996, is a mirror for the British influence in the islands.

5

Government

Bermuda has been a British colony since 1609. It has always had a high degree of self-government. It is, in fact, the oldest self-governing colony in the British Commonwealth. The colony has been making local laws ever since 1620, when its General Assembly met for the first time in the town of St. George.

Company Government

The Somers Islands Company ruled Bermuda until 1684. The Company appointed a Governor to represent its interests. It also provided for the election of a legislature composed of colonists. (A legislature is a body of persons given the responsibility and power to make laws for a country.) The governor had executive power, meaning he had the right to veto laws passed by the legislature. To the annoyance of the Bermudians, the company owners in London could veto a law accepted by the governor. The islanders were also displeased because the owners controlled aspects of their lives that affected company profits, such as the types of crops they could grow and the prices they could charge for the crops.

Nevertheless, the islanders had the right to decide many everyday details of life through the legislature. A land survey drew up boundaries of the legislative districts in the islands. The Company reserved St. George's and St. David's islands and a few smaller islands as company land. The Company divided the remainder of the land into eight parishes (called "tribes" then). It named each parish for a major owner of the Somers Islands Company: Hamilton, Smith's, Devonshire, Pembroke, Paget, Warwick, Southampton, and Sandys (pronounced Sandy by Bermudians). Landowning residents in each parish elected two representatives to a 16-member legislature.

Bermudians did not fare well under company rule. Nevertheless, the democratic form of government that it established has endured with a few changes during the entire history of the islands. The islanders have used their voice in government to make intelligent and effective decisions throughout the course of their history. Many such decisions were key to their economic survival on remote islands.

British Colonial Government

In 1684, Great Britain revoked the Somers Islands Company's charter. The British monarch took control by appointing a governor to the colony. The form of government was an old parliamentary system derived from the British Constitution of the seventeenth century. Bermudian land-holders elected members of a parliament. The parliament met to legislate laws and to make decisions about how to spend the colony's money. The parliament had a lower and an upper house and was answerable to the governor. In 1684, Bermuda's lower house had 36 members, 4 representatives from each of 9 parishes. (St. George's Parish, which included St. George's and St. David's islands, became the ninth parish.) The upper house was smaller, consisting of five members chosen by the governor and the lower house.

The Crown-appointed governor held executive authority. There was also a nominated council that served both as an advisory body to the governor and an upper house of parliament. The governor appointed judges to rule on legal disputes.

This parliamentary form of government changed very little in the colony for almost 300 years.

After the Second World War, Bermudians gained the right to vote, and they founded the first political parties. As islanders became more politically active, they began to seek a stronger parliament and more control of their country's affairs.

One of the greatest complaints about the political system was that a white male aristocracy held all the power. They usually made decisions that served their own interests. People who were not members of the parliament called this elite group the "Forty Thieves." The Forty Thieves were all descendants of groups of families that settled Bermuda. In early years of the colony, these families accumulated wealth as merchant mariners, privateers, and wreckers. After the maritime industry collapsed, they financed the shift first to agriculture and later on tourism. The Forty Thieves used their wealth to influence parliament as thoroughly as they influenced the economy.

Right to Vote

After the Second World War, Bermuda's long-held social and political preferences given to white males, at the expense of women and blacks, came under fire. Socially, whites segregated blacks. Segregation means to separate or set apart from others. Blacks had to eat in separate restaurants, dance only in black dance halls, and sit in certain sections of movie theaters. Politically, black men who owned land had the right to vote in the nineteenth century. Women, black and white, who owned land, did not receive the right to vote until 1944.

Theoretically, women and black men had the right to vote. However, few of them owned land. Making matters worse, property owners with property in more than one parish were allowed to cast two votes, the second vote was called a "plus vote." Since most property owners were white men, the plus vote gave this group even more power in deciding political elections.

In the mid-twentieth century, a series of events in Bermuda gave more blacks and all women the right to vote. In 1946, Dr. Edgar Fitzgerald Gordon, a Bermudian landowner with black Trinidadian and white Portuguese parents, was elected to the House of Assembly. He became the founder of a labor movement by organizing the first popular protests to call attention to the low wages and high cost of living in the islands.

Dr. Gordon's efforts laid the groundwork for the formation of trade unions in the 1950s. Trade unions, such as the Bermuda Industrial Union and the Dockworkers Union, had common interests. They wanted racial segregation to end and voting rights for everyone. Pressure for positive change quickly mounted. The dam of resistance finally broke in 1959, when Bermuda brought to an end racial segregation of theaters and dining and dancing halls. However, the law that gave property owners the plus-vote remained in effect.

Political Parties

In 1963, mostly black trade union members formed Bermuda's first political party, the Progressive Labor Party (PLP). In 1965, the majority of white voters and some blacks founded the United Bermuda Party (UBP). Since their beginning, these parties have emphasized different goals. The PLP was born from the labor movement of the 1950s. It is the liberal party, because it is concerned mainly with improving employment and wages. Most recently, the PLP has added Bermudian independence from the British Commonwealth as a goal. The UBP is the conservative party, because it focuses on promoting business, investment, and reducing taxes.

Constitution of 1968

Since the 1960s, the British government has had a lenient policy toward its colonies. It has allowed the colonies to hold elections to determine whether their citizens wish total independence from or continued membership in the British Commonwealth. If a colony chooses to remain in the Commonwealth, it may still reorganize its government as it sees fit, as long as the government is democratic and the British Monarch remains chief of state.

Although Bermuda chose to remain a Commonwealth colony, its newly formed political parties wanted more say in politics. In 1968, Bermuda's parliament adopted an amended Constitution that achieves that goal. This document is the basis for government in Bermuda today.

The Constitution of 1968 weakened the leadership role of governor and created the Office of the Premier. The Premier is the leader of the majority party and has the power to lead the government by working with a cabinet. The Premier has a strong role in appointing members of the cabinet. The Constitution also gives the minority party the power to form the parliamentary opposition.

The Constitution of 1968 also set up 20 election districts and allowed voters in each district to elect two representatives to the House of the Assembly. In 2002, the government amended the Constitution to increase the islands' electoral districts to 40. The government drew the boundaries of the newly created districts to include roughly the same number of voters. Under the new scheme, voters in each district elect a single representative to serve them in the House of the Assembly.

The constitution also guarantees that all adult citizens 18 years or older are eligible to vote. Previously, voting was limited to property owners. In addition, the constitution abolished the law that gave the plus-vote to property owners in favor of the principle of "one person-one vote."

Government Structure

Under the Constitution of 1968, the Bermuda Government has three main branches—Executive, Legislative, and Judicial. The executive branch has four components: chief of state, governor, premier, and cabinet. No one elects them. The chief of state is the British monarch, a hereditary position. The chief of state appoints a governor to represent Britain's interest in Bermuda. The governor shares control of Bermuda's police force with the Minister of Home Affairs. The governor is responsible for external affairs. He is in charge of the Bermuda Regiment, which is for external defense, and he works with the Premier in international negotiations affecting the islands.

Under the cabinet system, the British monarch invites the leader of the party with the most seats in parliament to form a government as premier. The premier is the head of government and leader of the majority party in the House of Assembly. He or she selects the cabinet, which is composed of 14 members, from among members of the House of Assembly and the Senate. The premier and cabinet are in complete charge of all aspects of government except foreign affairs, defense and internal security (including the police force).

The legislative branch is the parliament; it consists of the Senate and the House of Assembly. Bermudians elect the 40-member House for a term not to exceed five years. The purpose of the House is to make legislation that becomes law, usually after the Senate approves it. The government holds elections every five years, 2003 was the first scheduled in this century.

Members of the Senate are appointed, not elected. Senators serve concurrently with the House. The Senate has 11 members: five appointed by the governor in consultation with the premier, three by the opposition leader, and three at the governor's discretion. The Senate is a review body, meaning it does not make legislation. It reviews and recommends changes to legislation proposed by the House. However, most legislation must have final approval from the Senate before it becomes law.

The judicial branch administers the legal system. This branch consists of a Supreme Court and lower magistrate courts. The governor appoints all judges, including a Chief Justice to head the Supreme Court and judges in the magistrate court system.

Background to Party Politics

Bermuda held its first election based on equal voting rights in 1968. The UBP won 30 House of Assembly seats, whereas the PLP won 10. In the elections of 1972, 1976, and 1980, the UBP continued to control the government, though by decreasing margins in the Assembly.

In December 1977, a brief riot took place after the execution of two black men found guilty of the 1973 assassinations of Governor Sir Richard Sharples and four others. Although the riot took place in black neighborhoods, unsatisfied economic aspirations by young blacks, rather than racial tension, was its cause.

In the 1980s, increasing economic prosperity in Bermuda drew foreign workers into the islands. The growing population combined with limited land area, caused severe pressure in housing. In 1981, workers' unions called a general strike to protest housing and other economic conditions. In 1982, the ruling UBP elected Bermuda's first black premier—John Swain, a millionaire black businessman.

In 1995, discussions began regarding independence from the British Commonwealth. Swain, who had served as premier through several general elections, was strongly in favor of complete independence. In August 1995, an overwhelming majority (73%) of Bermudians voted against independence. Before the vote, Swain promised that he would resign if the vote were against independence. Swain fulfilled his promise and resigned. Ironically, following Swain's resignation, the opposition PLP added Bermuda's independence to its political goals.

Dr. David Saul, the Finance Minister, took Swain's place as Premier. Saul's administration was handicapped by the "McDonald's Hamburger" affair: Swain and one of Saul's cabinet members wanted to set up a McDonald's Restaurant in Bermuda. This issue was very controversial among Bermudians (see Chapter 4).

Eventually, the government passed a law that stopped the building of McDonald's or any similar chain restaurant on the islands. Since UBP members were involved in the McDonald's affair, opponents of Saul's administration pressured him to resign as Premier after two years in office in 1997. The UBP members elected Pamela Gordon, a daughter of the late E.F. Gordon (the former black labor leader), to replace Saul. Gordon was the first woman elected Premier, but not in a regular general election.

Recent Developments

Queen Elizabeth II has been the chief of state since 1952. Premier Jennifer Smith—a former Justice of the Peace, Member of Parliament, and leader of the Progressive Labor Party (PLP)—was the first woman elected premier in

The honorable Pamela Gordon (pictured here with former premier David Saul) was chosen the first woman premier of Bermuda by unanimous vote of the United Bermuda Party in 1997. Her father, the late E.F. Gordon, was renowned as a black labor leader and civil rights advocate.

a general election. Smith, who is black, entered office in the General Election of 1998, when the PLP won more House seats than the United Bermuda Party (UBP)—26 seats to 14 seats. The 1998 election was the first election the UBP lost in the 30 years of party voting. The PLP retained its control

Jennifer Smith, the first woman elected premier in a general election, is shown being sworn in at the Government house in 1998.

of the government in the 2003 election. Following the election, the more moderate Alex Scott replaced Jennifer Smith as premier and party leader.

The question of complete independence from the British Commonwealth is still a major political issue in Bermuda. Although the ruling PLP seeks complete independence, the majority of Bermudians do not. Bermuda's decision in 1995 to remain a colony is unusual as most colonies want political independence to open the door to economic prosperity or development. According to James Ahiakpor (1990), an economist, most Bermudians do not want independence because it bears certain costs. Bermuda would have to pay for a police force, administrating foreign policy (such as building embassies in other countries), and keeping a military. To

Bermuda's benefit, the United Kingdom takes care of all these things under current arrangements. Although the PLP wants complete independence, no one knows for sure if a majority of Bermudians will ever support it.

Bermuda's system of government has produced a politically and socially stable country, as occurrences of civil unrest have been very few throughout its entire history. As a result, the international community sees Bermuda as a reliable place for business, banking, investment, and tourism.

Tourism accounts for 28% of Bermuda's Gross Domestic Product and 40% percent of the tourists arrive on cruise ships. These ships typically spend a few days in port before moving on.

CHAPTER

6

Economy

T he people of Bermuda have one of the highest average incomes in the world. This fact seems remarkable given Bermuda's small size and history of economic struggle. However, today Bermuda exploits successfully its Atlantic location. It provides banking services for firms of other countries and luxury facilities for hundreds of thousands of tourists annually.

A global boom in tourism and international business and finance began during the mid-1900s, after the Second World War. As North America and Europe became more affluent, more and more members of middle and upper classes in these regions could afford to vacation elsewhere. Bermuda saw the potential of exploiting these markets. Bermudians built hotels, restaurants, and nightclubs for tourists. Bermuda also set up tax-free offshore bank accounts for corporations in the United States and Britain to transfer their businesses there.

Today, Bermuda's economy is creating so many jobs that non-Bermudians fill one in five jobs.

Although Bermuda boasts one of the highest average incomes in the world, a high cost of living burdens its citizens. Bermuda must also deal with lost revenues from the closure of military bases, competition in the tourist industry, health and pension costs of an aging population, and uncertainties of a global economy. This chapter focuses on successes, challenges, and uncertainties of Bermuda's economy.

Bermuda's Average Income

The United States Central Intelligence Agency (CIA) calculates a country's average income based on its gross domestic product (GDP). The GDP is the value of all final goods and services produced within a country in a given year. The average income is the income that each person in a country would have if each citizen were to receive an even share of the GDP.

According to the World Fact Book, a CIA publication, Bermuda, in 2000, had a GDP of $2.1 billion and an average income of $33,000. The average income is higher than the seven most industrialized countries in the world except the United States, which had an average income of $36,000 in 2000 (Table 3). The inflation rate based on Bermuda's consumer prices was only 2.7% in that year. Unemployment was almost nonexistent. Bermuda has three sources of income: primary and secondary industries, tourism, and international business. Using GDP data for 2000 from the World Fact Book, we will examine the three income sources.

Primary and Secondary Industries

Primary industries rely on direct use of land and natural resources to produce goods. In Bermuda, these industries include agriculture, fishing, and quarrying. Together, they employ only 1.5% of the labor force and produce about 3% of the GDP.

Agriculture, once an important sector in the economy,

Country	Average Income (U.S. Dollars)*
United States	36,200
Bermuda	**33,000**
Japan	24,900
Canada	24,800
France	24,400
Germany	23,400
United Kingdom	22,800
Italy	22,100

* Based on 2000 estimates of GDP
Source: Central Intelligence Agency, 2001

Table 3: Average Incomes for Bermuda and G7 Countries (seven most industrialized countries in the world)

barely survives today. Because of the sparseness of suitable land, only 600 acres, or about 4% of Bermuda's land, is under cultivation. Buildings and golf courses now occupy land where crops flourished before the Second World War. Nature preserves and private estates take up all remaining open space and prevent expansion of cultivated fields. The fields that do exist are small plots scattered around the larger islands.

About 80% of Bermuda's food needs are imported. Bermuda imports fresh meat from the United States, produce from the United States and Canada, and dairy products and goods from a variety of countries, including the United States, Canada, United Kingdom, Ireland, and New Zealand. There is considerable egg and dairy production, however. Bermuda also produces some onions, potatoes, and green vegetables. Subtropical fruits, such as bananas, papayas, oranges, and grapefruit, also are grown. There is some production of flowers for the local market. Easter lily bulbs and flowers are the only agricultural exports.

Bermuda has a reef fishery and an offshore fishery. The reef fishery is home primarily to shallow water groupers, snappers, and jacks. The offshore fishery consists of primarily deep-water marlin, wahoo, large tuna, sharks, and dolphin fish (not the dolphin mammal). In the 1960s, these fisheries provided two-thirds of all fish consumed in Bermuda. However, owing largely to overfishing, by the early 1980s, the consumption of local fish declined to one-third and the tastier "white-meat" varieties—grouper and snapper—were threatened with extinction.

In 1990, a fish pot ban to preserve the fish supply in reef areas drove many fishermen out of business. Fish pots trap all sorts of fish, which sometimes die before fishermen return to collect them and to release overfished varieties. Because of the ban, income from fishing contributes a small amount of income to Bermuda's GDP.

Quarrying rocks for making construction materials also has a minor impact on the GDP. There are only two large rock quarries in the islands—both in Hamilton Parish. Somerset Parish has several small quarries. Workers dig up the limestone, and then use saws to cut it into blocks of stone. The blocks harden when exposed to air. Before they harden, workers cut some blocks into tiles. Whitewashing the tiles with lime makes them impermeable to water and ideal roofing material. Workers crush some of the limestone for cement production. Construction companies purchase these limestone products to construct homes and buildings. Quarrying employs only a few dozen people, because there is not much land available for new construction.

Secondary industries are industries that add value to other products. Such industries usually involve assembling raw materials and manufacturing. Secondary industry accounts for only 3.2% of Bermuda's jobs and 17% of its GDP. The main secondary industries on the islands are the manufacture of concentrated essences (perfumes), pharmaceutical products, and beauty preparations. Beer brewing, carbonated beverages bottling, cedar wood production, paint manufacture, glass blowing, and ornamental iron working also produce some income.

Tourism

During the second half of the twentieth century, tourist dollars became a cornerstone of Bermuda's economy. In earlier years, when travel was by slow steamer, the islands were one of the closest warm destinations for winter vacationers from Canada and the northeastern United States. After the Second World War, Bermuda's high season for tourism switched to spring, summer, and autumn. This switch occurred because air travel enabled winter vacationers to travel farther south to islands in the West Indies, such as the Bahamas, Barbados, Jamaica, and Puerto Rico.

Tourism now accounts for 28% of Bermuda's GDP. When tourists come to the islands, either they stay onboard cruise ships or they check into hotels. They dine out and dance, lie on the beach, play tennis and golf, swim, body surf, snorkel, scuba dive, water ski, windsurf, sail, fish, hike, bird watch, ride mopeds and bicycles, take taxis, go sightseeing, visit historical sites, and buy souvenirs and artworks. The needs and activities of tourists create thousands more jobs than international business does. Tourism creates 3,500 jobs directly and perhaps twice that number indirectly.

Bermuda is a high-quality but very high-cost destination. More than 450,000 visitors come per year. Most visit in April through October, and most are 35 years old or older. They usually have college degrees and modest incomes. Repeat visitors tend to be wealthier and to stay longer. Tourists come primarily from the United States (84%), Canada (8%), and the United Kingdom (4%). About half of the remaining 4% come from continental Europe.

Gombey dancing reminds Bermudians of their African heritage. The tradition of gombey dancers dates back to at least the mid-1700s. On holidays they typically take their dances to the streets of Hamilton.

Bermuda is just two hours by air from New York City. Therefore, 60% of Bermuda's half-million visitors arrive by airliner. Air travelers stay an average of six days. They spend most of their money on expensive hotel rooms. The remaining 40% of Bermuda's tourists arrives aboard cruise ships. Cruise ship travelers spend less money than airline travelers do. Cruise ship travelers average three days in the country and stay on ships rather than in expensive Bermudian hotels.

Bermuda's tourism industry peaked in the late 1980s. The number of annual visitors then was about 650,000. In those days, more tourists were "big-spender" air travelers. Recently, income from tourism has been declining. An average of about 450,000 tourists were coming to Bermuda in the early 2000s. They were spending less money because more of them were arriving by cruise ship. The decline in tourist dollars has forced several luxury hotels to close since 1988. The main cause of the decline in tourism has been increasing competition from the West Indies.

International Business

International businesses relocate to Bermuda for one primary reason: Bermuda does not make them pay corporate income and capital gains taxes. Since their official residence is in Bermuda, these companies' earnings are not subject to taxes in their home countries either. Bermudian-owned businesses and individuals, on the other hand, are not exempt from taxes. Other reasons international businesses relocate to Bermuda are geographical location, excellent telecommunications and phone service, political stability, and advanced computer technology.

Every year since in 1992, international businesses have earned more income than tourism has. Therefore, Bermuda's economy has continued to grow despite tourism's slump because of money from international businesses. In 2001, these businesses accounted for about 60% of Bermuda's economic output.

Bermuda benefits from being a tax haven to international businesses in two ways. First, companies pay various fees to Bermuda's banks for holding their money and making financial transactions for them. Second, these companies employ Bermudians. Moreover, Bermudian companies that work with international businesses must hire additional person-nel. Bermudians understand the importance of attracting international businesses to their shores. Indeed, Bermuda's fear of scaring away foreign firms is part of the reason why the independence vote in late 1995 failed.

Bermuda's international businesses include mutual funds services, investment holding firms, and insurance companies that specialize in reinsurance. Reinsurance is a type of catastrophic insurance that protects conventional insurers against natural disasters. Bermuda's income from commercial insurance and reinsurance businesses now ranks alongside the incomes of New York and London from these businesses.

About 275 international businesses from all over the world have physically moved offices to Bermuda to avoid paying taxes in their home countries. Another 14,500 companies do not pay taxes in their home countries by simply declaring post office boxes in Bermuda as their address.

International companies must conduct their business outside Bermuda. They must also follow regulatory guidelines of the Bermuda Monetary Authority (BMA). The BMA is the government agency that oversees all financial activities in the country. According to the British government, the BMA has put in place strong regulations to deter criminal abuse, such as laundering drug money through international businesses.

Service-Oriented Economy

Bermuda's economy is primarily a service-oriented economy, because nearly 90% of its income (GDP) comes from providing services. Service economies are typical of high-income countries. The term "white collar" describes jobs in the service sector. Economists rate white-collar jobs "highly skilled" compared with jobs in industry. (The term "blue collar" describes occupations in industry.) Bermuda's service economy provides financial services for international firms and hotel, restaurant, and recreation facilities to tourists.

Tourism and international finance and business accounted for 38.7% of all jobs in 1994. Hotels, restaurants, and international businesses account for most of these jobs.

Women fill more than 80% of clerical jobs, and black women have the majority of these. Women also hold more jobs than men do in professional, technical, and related fields. However, men hold the majority of jobs (62%) in administrative and managerial positions. White men outnumber black men in this category three to one.

Large Trade Deficit

Bermuda has a large trade deficit. A trade deficit occurs when the value of a country's imports is greater than that of its exports. The value of Bermuda's imported goods is astronomical compared with the value of its exports. In 2000, according to the World Bank, exports equaled $56 million and imports $739 million. The balance is minus $683 million. In other words, the amount of money spent for imports was 13 times greater than the amount of income received for exports!

Bermuda's small land area limits its natural resource base and what it can produce. As a result, the colony must import a large proportion of its food, clothing, fuel, and other necessities. Most of these supplies come from the United States and the United Kingdom. The islands' main exports are essences of perfumes and re-export items, such as pharmaceuticals and fuels and supplies for ships that stop over at the port in Hamilton.

Closure of Military Bases

After the Second World War, Bermuda lost revenue when the military-related operations of outside countries began closing. Final closures took place in 1995, after the end of the Cold War. Three countries have had bases in Bermuda. They are England, Canada, and the United States. Before their departure, these countries were paying money to Bermuda to lease the bases. Base personnel were also providing cash and sales tax revenue by spending money on consumer items.

In 1951, Great Britain closed its largest facility, the Dockyard, which was a ship repair yard on North Ireland Island. In 1995, Britain also closed its naval and army facilities on Boaz, Watford, and North and South Ireland islands. Two years earlier, Canada, closed its wireless tracking station at Daniel's Head in Somerset, Sandys Parish.

The United States had the largest wartime and Cold War presence; it operated the Great Sound Naval Air Station in Sandys Parish, a submarine listening post at Tudor Hill in Southampton Parish, the Kindley Air Force Base on St. David's Island in St. George's Parish, and a National Aeronautics and Space Administration (NASA) satellite tracking station. The United States turned over the last of these bases to civilian usage in 1995.

Bermuda has raised taxes in recent years, partly because of lost revenue from closure of military bases. For example, during the early 1990s, the Bermuda Government was receiving about $60 million dollars each year from property leases to the United States bases.

High Cost of Living

Living in Bermuda is very expensive. Most families must have three incomes to cover expenses. For example, a husband might work full time as a skilled tradesman and part time as a taxi driver, while his wife might work full time as a sales clerk. There are two main reasons for the high cost of living: high prices for consumer goods and high housing costs.

Nearly everything eaten, worn, and used in Bermuda is imported. The cost of transporting consumer goods from other countries, primarily from the United States and Canada, doubles and triples prices.

Prices are even higher because the Bermuda Government's single biggest source revenue is taxes on imported goods. (Governments depend on taxes to pay for essential services for citizens, such as police and fire protection, street building and maintenance, and schools.) Bermuda's taxes on imports boost the retail prices of such goods as much as 33%.

Comparing prices of imports in Bermuda with prices of the same goods in the United States is interesting. Bermuda prices for appliances such as dishwashers, televisions, and refrigerators are twice U.S. prices. Gasoline is four times U.S. gasoline prices. Personal care items such as deodorant, toothpaste, and shampoo are three times U.S. prices. Prices of household goods such as pet food and paper towels are also three times U.S. prices.

Costs of consumer items produced in Bermuda are more reasonable. Milk, cream, ice cream, eggs, and some vegetables have prices similar to those in the United States. Bermudians must also pay a huge annual license fee for cars. Depending on the car model, the fee ranges up to $1,100.

High home and rental prices also raise the cost of living in Bermuda. There are two reasons for high home and rental prices. First, there is a high demand for existing residences, but hardly any of them are unoccupied. Consequently, profit-minded owners are inclined to sell or rent available residences at very high prices. The second reason for the high cost of housing is the shortage of land on which to build new houses and apartments. Landowners are therefore in a position to charge very high prices to builders for their land. To recover the money they spend on land, builders raise the purchase price of the homes and rentals they build.

Many densely settled countries and cities in the world build tall condominiums and apartment buildings, so that more people can live on less land. However, Bermuda must protect its natural beauty so that tourists will continue coming. As a result, the government has laws that limit the heights of buildings to protect the natural look of its islands.

The price of an average-size home in Bermuda is at least three times the average price of the same home in the United

States. As a result, few Bermudians can afford to purchase homes. For example, in 1999, only about 45% of Bermudians owned their own homes, compared with 67% in the United States. A modest single-family three-bedroom home that might cost $160,000 in the United States costs at least $1 million in Bermuda.

Most Bermudians rent apartments because they cannot afford to purchase expensive houses or condominiums. Since the same inflationary pressures that affect prices of homes also affect the costs of rents, the Bermuda Government applies rent controls to keep rents down. Almost one-half of Bermuda's rental units have rent controls. Nevertheless, rents are still high; the minimum rent for a two-bedroom apartment is at least four times as much for a similar apartment in the United States.

Bermuda's smallness also prevents many non-Bermudians from purchasing vacation property there. Non-Bermudians, who do not have a Bermudian spouse, may purchase only one residential property. The government requires that the property must be one of Bermuda's most expensive single-family residences.

In general, properties sold to non-Bermudians have price tags of more than $2 million. If a foreigner agrees to purchase such a property, he or she must also pay a fee of 22% on the value of the property. Add on the annual land tax in Bermuda, which is about five times greater than the U.S. property tax, and you can see why only the wealthiest foreigners can afford to buy a vacation home in Bermuda!

Aging Population and Future Tax Increases

Like other wealthy nations, Bermuda tries to help its older people live out their final years comfortably. Bermuda's assistance includes partial payments for retirees' health care and pensions. Population pyramids for 2000, 2025, and 2050 illustrate how Bermuda has an aging population. The pyramid for 2000 shows a "bulge" among 30- to 65-year-olds. In economic terms, the 30- to 65-year age group is the most productive group. They tend to be highly skilled. They also earn more money and pay more taxes than other age groups.

Bermuda's 2025 and 2050 population pyramids show that fewer and fewer people will be paying taxes, as today's bulge of productive taxpayers move into less productive retirement years. Moreover, older people will be living longer. Thus, the government's pension and health care costs for older people will be rising in the future. The government will have to pay for these costs by raising taxes, on income, property, business, or imported goods, or some combination of these.

Economic Uncertainties

Tourism and international banking and finance, the two primary contributors to Bermuda's GDP, depend on the strength of other nation's economies. Thus, what affects the world, affects Bermuda a great deal. This fact creates a high degree of uncertainty about the country's future. The global economy is slowing down after a period of unprecedented growth in the 1990s. Until the economy picks up, there will be fewer people able to pay for vacations in luxury class destinations such as Bermuda. There also will be fewer business transactions and therefore less income from international businesses.

In addition, the ongoing global war on terrorism is having a negative impact on international business and tourism, but especially on tourism. Where American tourists choose to vacation was deeply affected by the terrorist attack on the World Trade Towers in New York City and the Pentagon near Washington, D.C., on September 11, 2001. Since terrorists used airliners in the attack, people are understandably cautious about traveling on airliners to popular American tourist spots such as Bermuda. It is difficult to say how much and for how long the war on terrorism will affect Bermuda's economy.

Because of the scarcity of surface water conserving rainfall takes a high priority for residents. This roof is terraced to drain rainwater into underground water storage tanks.

Living in Bermuda Today

Mark Twain once called Bermuda "a little island paradise." A hundred years later, hardly anyone will disagree with his assessment of Bermuda's beauty: It still has, as Twain said, "breezy groves, flower gardens, coral caves and lovely vistas of blue water." Nevertheless, living in Bermuda today is also very different from living in Bermuda in Twain's day. The islands are more crowded. Perhaps as important, the tourist economy has quickened the pace of life; there are now expensive restaurants, late-night bars, nightclubs, hotels, and a more international "feel" to the place.

Bermudians are friendly and gracious to tourists, and they are accepting of tourism's influence. Nevertheless, they have their own lifestyle and prefer to spend little time in the tourist scene. This chapter examines aspects of Bermuda's lifestyle: social clubs, homes, dress, food, education, health, communications media, and transportation.

Social Clubs

In their spare time, islanders choose to be with their families and to join private social clubs so that they can relax and interact with other Bermudians. Social clubs have been a prominent feature of Bermuda's social landscape for many decades.

Islanders have formed yacht clubs, civic clubs, sports associations, charitable organizations, historical and literary societies, philatelic (postage stamp) societies, garden clubs, kennel clubs, dramatic societies, and other groups. Membership in such clubs is open to all races. Social position, which depends on one's occupation, education, or economic standing, is the basis for membership, not race. There are also clubs for non-Bermudians who work in or own vacation homes in Bermuda. Bermudians are very sports-minded, so sports' associations are the most widespread social clubs; they sponsor various sports teams and raise money for payment of uniforms, equipment, and playing fields.

Social clubs, especially, are important in keeping Bermudians on the islands. In *Black Clubs in Bermuda,* Frank Manning wrote:

In Bermuda, as a small place, the outlet is very limited. There's [sic] only a few things you can do. You could become active in these clubs, or turn around and just hang around the bars or something like that. It's not too much to do in Bermuda. It's very small. You don't have the outlet like other parts of the world, where if you didn't belong to a club you could go somewhere weekends, out of state or something, and find other interests . . . If I hadn't been in club life, I probably would have ventured to go abroad.

Homes

Many homes of islanders bear the stamp of English architecture and Bermudian ingenuity. These homes are similar to the small English cottage. However, Bermuda limestone is the primary construction material. Shallow quarries in backyards are often the source of the limestone. These cottage-size homes are usually one or two stories tall and have high-pitched, gabled roofs. Windows on both sides balance their front doors. Chimneys for wood-burning fireplaces are typical.

The roof of Bermudian homes is an adaptation to the sparseness of the islands' water supply. Surface water for drinking is nonexistent because of the porosity of limestone bedrock, and saltwater contamination of drinkable groundwater is a concern. Resourceful Bermudians "terrace" their roofs with limestone tiles to drain rainwater into underground water storage tanks. A law requires homes have terraced roofs and storage tanks.

Bermuda also has laws requiring roofs be whitewashed with lime to help purify the collected rainwater. Laws also mandate that all homes be painted in traditional pastel hues (such as aqua, lavender, pink, and turquoise) to help preserve the historical flavor of the islands.

Imported concrete block is the primary construction material of new homes, because local limestone quarries have been unable to keep up with demand and local limestone is more expensive. Concrete blocks might be less expensive, but they are inferior to porous limestone. Heat conducts through dense concrete quickly, so newer homes tend to be too warm in summer and too cool in winter.

Water Supply

Water supply is a big concern to people living in Bermuda. Scientists who study climate classify Bermuda's climate as moist. A moist climate has a lot of water remaining after subtracting the amount of water lost through evaporation. Nevertheless, the colony's water supply is not great, because there are no permanent streams. Moreover, water is not drinkable in the few lakes that exist because it is too salty. Bermuda has three main sources of fresh (drinkable) water. They are rainfall, groundwater, and desalination works.

Rainfall is the main source of fresh water. As previously described, tiled roofs drain rainwater into storage tanks beneath homes. A home's water supply stays in the tank until it is used. Turning on a facet or flushing a toilet starts an electric pump that draws water from the tank and into the home.

Groundwater is the second most important source of fresh water. A large aquifer (a porous layer of underground rock that stores water) sits under Bermuda. Undrinkable seawater seeps into the aquifer. However, in certain places freshwater from rainfall seeps into the aquifer in large amounts. The freshwater zones in the aquifer are called *lenses*. Water company wells tap into the lenses and pump the water into large storage tanks. The water companies deliver the well water in trucks to the homes when there is a drought and storage tanks in homes are empty.

Desalinated (desalted) water is Bermuda's third most important water source. Removing salts from brackish water (a mixture of fresh and salt water) and seawater makes water drinkable. This desalination process requires expensive equipment, so desalinated water is expensive to make. Nevertheless, many big businesses in Bermuda do not have large enough rainwater storage tanks. These businesses use a lot of water and are willing to pay for desalinated water. Many of these users receive desalinated water from underground water pipes, rather than by truck delivery. Large hotels especially depend on desalinated water.

Dress

Generally, Bermudians dress as people do in the United States and in Europe, except for one item of men's clothing—Bermuda shorts. The shorts, which have a nearly knee-length style, got their start in the early twentieth century, when British soldiers in outposts with hot climates trimmed the legs of their khaki trousers to be more comfortable in the heat. (Khaki is a tan-colored tightly woven cotton fabric.) British officers paid tailors in Bermuda to do the same thing.

Bermuda shorts have become emblematic of Bermuda's people, yet their origin was humble. When British soldiers were posted to tropical climates they simply cut off their trousers to keep cool.

These khaki shorts quickly became a local trademark in Bermuda after the tailors began selling them to civilians. Today, Bermuda shorts (in a variety of colors) are standard wear for conservatively dressed professionals, such as male teaches, bankers, and insurance executives. In addition to the shorts, formal male dress includes socks that reach just below the knees, a dress shirt, tie and jacket. It is preferred that the shorts and jacket be of different colors and that socks have colors that go with either the shorts or the jacket.

Island Cuisine

There are no Big-Macs or Whoppers in Bermuda. In 1999, the Bermuda Legislature passed a law banning fast-food restaurants, such as McDonald's and Burger King. The ban is popular with Bermudians, because they feel that big fast-food outlets owned by international corporations do not fit well with the uniqueness and charm of their small islands. Only a lone outlet exists; Bermuda passed the fast-food ban after Kentucky Fried Chicken had already built a restaurant on the islands.

Only a few everyday dishes are exclusively Bermudian cuisine. British, West Indian, and American cultures influence most meals eaten by islanders. The two most common truly Bermudian dishes are Bermudian fish chowder and fish sandwiches (which are as popular in Bermuda as hamburgers in the United States). Mussel pie, shark hash, and Bermuda spiny lobster are also popular with local residents. A traditional Sunday family meal is a codfish breakfast, which consists of salt cod, eggs, boiled Irish potatoes, bananas, avocado, and a sauce of onions and potatoes. On certain days of the year, such as Good Friday, codfish cake is cooked. This dish was more important in the Bermudian diet in the past. A customary Christmas dish is cassava pie, which is made of meat filling and grated pieces of the root from the cassava plant.

Education

Education is free and required of all children ages 5 through 16. Nearly 10% of Bermudians older than age 16 have a college diploma, and 98% can read and write. The public school and private school systems are similar. Children begin with six years of primary schooling (including kindergarten), three years at middle school and four years at the secondary or high school level. The school year begins in early September and lasts 10 months. There are breaks at Christmas, at Easter, and during the summer. Graduates of both public and private schools may prepare for further studies at either Bermuda College (two-year, junior college) or postsecondary schools abroad. Most students choose to attend colleges and universities in the United States, Canada, or England.

Uniforms are mandatory in all of Bermuda's schools, from kindergarten through senior secondary school. The color of skirt, jacket, trousers, and tie identify each school. In this way, Bermuda practices the British custom of having children wear uniforms to school. Despite the fact that there are many schools in Bermuda to choose from, many wealthy families still send their children to expensive private boarding schools in America, Canada, or the United Kingdom. About 1,200 children or 10% of all school-aged children attend such schools.

Health

Overall, Bermudians are a very healthy people. The average life expectancy for women is around 79 years, and for men, around 75 years. Bermuda may be small in size and population, but it has excellent health care facilities. There are two hospitals, both of which are government-maintained. The first deals with general health; the second focuses on mental health. Because Bermuda is a British dependent territory, overseas visitors sometimes assume that its citizens have a free national health plan like that in the United Kingdom. This is not true. Bermudian citizens and their employers pay taxes for employee health care insurance. The government also operates several public health clinics that can treat a variety of minor illnesses and injuries. Treatment at the clinics is free for citizens, although medicines are not.

Communications, Media, and Roads

Bermuda's leading newspaper is the *Royal Gazette*. It has both national and international news. The Internet has a scaled-down version of it at *www.accessbda.bm*. Because of the large number of tourists on the islands, one can find a wide range of international newspapers. Bermuda also has cable television, which includes all of the major United States networks (ABC, CBS, CNN, Fox, HBO, NBC, and PBS) as well as the British Broadcasting Company (BBC). Two radio stations broadcast all kinds of music, including country and western, rock, and contemporary.

Bermuda's road system consists of about 180 miles (290 kilometers) of paved and unpaved roads. Public roads connect larger islands by bridges. About half the roads are private. Most roads are near the two main towns, Hamilton and St. George's. The maximum speed limit is just 20 mph (30 km per hour) because the roads are narrow and have many sharp curves. This low speed limit slows considerably the pace of life on the islands. Drivers caught speeding must pay heavy fines. Driving under the influence of alcohol or drugs brings stiff penalties; offenders cannot legally drive for at least one year, in addition to paying a heavy fine.

Automobiles

Bermudians have not developed a "love affair with their cars" as Americans have done. They know that their islands are too small and their roads too narrow for many cars. In 1906, an American Newspaper owner named James Gordon Bennett brought the first automobile to Bermuda on a steamboat. In those days, these "horseless carriages" were new and unusual. Henry Ford built the first such machine just three years earlier in Michigan. These motor-driven carriages had no mufflers, so they were very noisy. Bermudians were said to be amazed, even spooked, when Bennett drove his newfangled motorcar noisily down the islands' rutted carriage roads. They thought his automobile was too noisy for their quiet islands, and they thought using horses and boats for transportation on small islands made good sense.

Many regular visitors to Bermuda agreed. Two of the islands' most famous visitors, Mark Twain and Woodrow

Wilson, who would become President of the United States in 1912, led a popular campaign to banish automobiles from Bermuda. As a result, early in 1910, the Bermuda Legislature passed a law that banned Bennett's and any future automobiles from the islands. This ban would last more than three and a half decades, during which time the rest of the Western world became very dependent on driving "horseless carriages."

World War II brought about pressures to end the automobile ban. Before the war, horses were still the primary means of transportation on the islands. Cargo ships would bring hay and oats for horses to eat. During the war, things began to change. Fewer cargo ships visited Bermuda, because they had to carry supplies, war materials, and troops to Europe. As the war continued, Bermudians were finding it difficult to feed their horses. Moreover, the American military was in Bermuda, and it needed roads and automobiles for its operations there. Bermuda officially canceled its ban of automobiles in 1946, one year after the war ended.

From the beginning of their usage, Bermuda's Ministry of Transport has restricted the size and number of automobiles. Each family may own only one passenger car. All such cars must be small, no longer than 14 feet (4.3 meters). Therefore, Bermudians drive small sedans, hatchbacks, or station wagons. Only businesses may own trucks.

The Ministry of Transport does not allow tourists to rent passenger cars, since more cars would increase traffic and pollution problems. However, visitors 16 years or older may rent mopeds (motorized bicycles) or small scooters for excursions. Since the speed limit is only 20 mph (30 km per hour), both visitors and residents find that bicycles, mopeds, or small motor scooters are good means of transportation. For safety, helmets are required of both drivers and passengers. In many instances, since the islands are so small, people are able to walk to and from their destinations. Passenger buses are another means of transportation. Buses are especially small to suit Bermuda's narrow roads; they are so small that there is no room for suitcases or baby strollers. During the tourist season, these small buses are frequently crowded with tourists as well as local residents. Taxis and passenger ferries also operate in the islands.

The government's efforts to limit the size and number of automobiles have not been a total success. There is still some traffic congestion in and around Hamilton, the capital, just before the workday begins and ends. In addition to traffic congestion, air pollution from motor exhaust is becoming a growing concern on the islands.

Airport and Railroad

The Bermuda International Airport is located on St. David's Island, where the United States Air Force base used to be. The Bermuda government owns and operates it. All types of aircraft can land and take off from there. Passenger airlines operate more flights a day during the tourist season. Cities served via direct flights are Atlanta, Baltimore, Boston, Charlotte, Halifax, London, Newark, New York, Philadelphia, and Toronto.

Because of Bermuda's strategic location the airport also handles military flights, including those of the Egyptian Air Force, which uses Bermuda regularly as a refueling base, and aircraft of the Royal Air Force, Royal Canadian Air Force, Saudi Air Force, United States Air Force, United States Coast Guard, and United States Navy.

There is no railroad in Bermuda, although the government built a railway and operated a small train from 1931 to 1947. The train stopped running because it never gained popularity as a method of transportation. In 1984, the government set aside sections of the old railway route for hiking and horseback riding enthusiasts. Together, these sections makeup the Railway Trail: it is 21 miles in length and runs from Somerset Village at the west end of Bermuda to the town of St. George's at east end of the colony. The trail is a popular getaway destination for both Bermudians and tourists.

Land-based Sports and Leisure

Bermudians like the outdoors. Throughout the year, the islands' warm, sunny weather draws them outdoors to watch or to participate in various sporting events. Many social clubs exist primarily to organize team sports and other pastimes. These activities take place on both land and sea.

Cricket, soccer, and rugby—introduced by the British—are the most popular land-based sports. Bermudians select all-star teams in these sports to compete in international tournaments. Bermudians are tough competitors. For example, in 1996 and 1998, the Bermuda Rugby team won the Caribbean Rugby Championship.

Islanders enjoy many other land-based pastimes. Tennis is very popular and has been for a long time. England introduced it to the islands in 1873. Bermudians introduced the game to the United States one year later. Playing field hockey is another favorite pastime. Teams play field hockey on a hard surface rather than on ice and with a hockey ball instead of a puck.

Bermudians play baseball, too. U.S. military personnel stationed in Bermuda introduced the sport to islanders in the 1940s. The game is now very popular, especially among young people. Several dozen teams play baseball as an organized sport on just two baseball diamonds.

Bermudians also have a custom of flying kites. On most weekends, multicolored kites, many locally made, fly lazily over the islands' shorelines. Good Friday is a public holiday and traditionally a kite-flying day. Islanders also participate in or are spectators of harness racing, squash, golf, volleyball, and basketball.

Water-based Sports and Leisure

Bermudians engage in many water-related activities, both as spectators and as participants. They enjoy swimming, sail

The Newport-Bermuda sailing regatta is a 650-mile yacht race that draws yacht enthusiasts from around the world.

boating, deep-sea fishing, shore (surf) fishing, parasailing, scuba diving, kayaking, skiing, snorkeling, and windsurfing. Many of these activities are also popular with tourists.

Islanders are famous for yacht racing. Almost every weekend these large sailboats glide swiftly and silently across open waters of the Great Sound. Bermudian yacht clubs hold many races there. Bermudian yacht crews also compete against sailors from around the world. These international races begin each spring during International Race Week and continue throughout the summer. In early summer on every even-numbered year, the main nautical event is the 650-mile Newport-to-Bermuda yacht race. Yacht enthusiasts from all over the world also enter this race, which begins in Newport, Rhode Island, and ends in St. George's Harbour.

Bermudians also like to race small dinghies. A dinghy is an unusual sailboat that British military officers stationed in Bermuda designed in the late 1800s. Great skill is required to keep this boat upright because of its top-heavy frame; it is only 14 feet, 1-inch (4.3 meters) long, but its mast towers 40 feet (12.2 meters) high.

Dinghy races are always fun to watch, because the boats are so difficult to sail at high speeds. During races, the unstable dinghies are pitched up and down and sideways by the waves and wind. Their crews must jump crazily back and forth from port (left-side) to starboard (right-side) to keep the boat from tipping over. Although dinghy races can be hilarious to watch, the racers are very serious about winning. For instance, to lighten the dinghy for added speed, crewmembers may even leap overboard. Do they wear life jackets? No!

A street in St. George's Parish is a typical narrow, winding alleyway with pastel-tinted buildings on either side.

8

Bermuda Looks Ahead

A s a tiny group of islands 650 miles from the nearest mainland, Bermuda's existence depends on outside input. The country is a colony of the United Kingdom. It also depends heavily on imports for everything from food to machinery. That Bermudians have survived so well is a tribute to their taking advantage of an Atlantic location.

As seafarers in the North Atlantic, Bermuda's inhabitants survived as ship builders and traders in the eighteenth and nineteenth centuries. In hard times, they resorted to wrecking, smuggling, privateering, and blockade running. The twentieth century brought improvements to sea and air transportation. As a result, Bermuda turned to exporting vegetables and attracting tourists. Most recently, the colony thrust itself into world prominence as a pioneer of offshore banking and finance. Today, Bermuda's GDP is very high for its small population, and unemployment is rare.

Bermuda has many qualities that are very attractive to tourists and business executives. It stands out among nations because it has one of the highest average annual incomes in the world. The country has adequate education, health, transportation, and communication facilities. The people are friendly and engage in activities that bring them together socially and culturally. Bermuda is a politically stable nation as well. In addition, the colony has a slow-paced lifestyle, charming landscapes, and natural beauty. All these factors combine to make Bermuda an attractive place for banking, investment, and tourism.

Bermuda faces challenges in the future, as all nations do. As Bermuda looks ahead, it must deal with three fundamental problems—a housing shortage, an aging population, and global economic competition. The first two problems are making living in Bermuda increasingly expensive. Bermuda needs more housing to relieve population overcrowding. However, there is virtually no land on which to build more homes. Bermuda could allow high-rise apartments and condominiums so that more people could live on less land. Alternatively, it could fill in shallow lagoon areas to create new land for more one-story and two-story homes. Both of these policies would result in more homes, but both would lessen the islands' natural beauty and thereby drive away tourists and tourist-related jobs. Thus, the housing shortage and the high cost of housing that this shortage causes are likely to continue.

Bermuda's aging population is also a challenge to its future. Because its population is getting older, Bermuda will probably have to raise taxes to help pay for health care, retirement pensions, and a shrinking income tax base. Higher taxes will raise even more the cost of living in Bermuda.

The nature of Bermuda's role in the global economy will also affect its future. Bermudians have a history of self-reliance and independence. These qualities enabled them to take advantage of Bermuda's mid-Atlantic location. However, in the global economy, economic growth depends increasingly on cooperation rather than on independent action. Countries are joining regional economic alliances to compete in this economy. The European Economic Community (EEC) and the North American Free Trade Association (NAFTA) are two examples. Former Premier Jennifer Smith expressed the importance of Bermuda's participation in the global economy in the following quote:

> The world is changing and we must change with it. Today, living in isolation, separate and apart from the global economy, is not a recipe for success. Globalization and the increasing tendency toward regional and hemispheric links make it not only prudent, but also necessary, for countries to form partnerships that foster their mutual interests. (Regan 2001).

Bermuda's first economic partnership went into effect in 2003, when the country became a member of the Caribbean Community (CARICOM). CARICOM promotes inter-regional trade among member countries. In 2003, Bermuda also began talks with Cuba to set up cultural exchanges. When such exchanges occur, they would allow scholars, writers, and artists to visit each other's countries in order to share views and ideas. Additional economic and cultural ties between Bermuda and the Caribbean region seems likely, as Bermuda and the Caribbean islands have similar colonial experiences and value systems, as well as similar population and economic problems. These similarities should make it easier for Bermuda and the Caribbean islands to work together toward common solutions.

Facts at a Glance

Land and People

Official Name	Bermuda
Location	Bermuda is located in the northern Atlantic Ocean about 650 miles (1,050 kilometers) east of South Carolina (US).
Area	22.7 square miles (58.8 square kilometers)
Climate	Subtropical; mild and humid
Capital	Hamilton
Other Towns or Villages	St. George (town) and Somerset and Flatt's villages
Population	64,935 (July 2004 estimate)
Population Density	2,991 persons per square mile (1,154 per square kilometer)
Major Rivers	None
Mountains	None (Low hills separated by fertile depressions)
Languages	English (official), Portuguese
Religions	Non-Anglican Protestant 39%, Anglican 27%, Roman Catholic 15%, other 19%
Literacy	98%

Economy

Natural Resources	Limestone, pleasant climate fostering tourism
Agricultural Products	Bananas, papayas, oranges, grapefruits, vegetables, eggs, citrus, flowers, Easter lily bulbs, dairy products
Industries	Tourism, finance, insurance, quarrying, structural concrete products, fishing, paints, perfumes, pharmaceuticals, beauty preparations, ship repairing
Major Imports	Machinery, transport equipment, construction materials, chemicals, food and live animals
Major Exports	Easter lily bulbs, flowers and re-exports of pharmaceuticals
Currency	Bermudian dollar

Government

Form of Government	Parliamentary British overseas territory with parliamentary democracy that includes a Premier, Cabinet, Senate and House of Assembly
Government Bodies	Executive, legislative, and judicial branches
Formal Head of State	Monarch of England represented by a governor
Voting Rights	All citizens over the age of 18 can vote.

1503 Juan de Bermudez, the captain of a Spanish vessel, discovers Bermuda.

1603 Diego Ramirez, a Spanish galleon captain, spends three weeks on the island repairing his vessel. Upon returning to Seville, Spain, he delivers a description and map of the islands to his superiors.

1609 The English vessel *Sea Venture,* wrecks on the reefs of Bermuda. All 150 persons on board successfully make it to shore, including Sir George Somers, the ship's captain. Somers claims Bermuda as an English possession.

1610 The shipwrecked colonizers leave Bermuda and sail on to Virginia. Somers leaves two men in Bermuda, the islands' first permanent inhabitants.

1612 The King of England gives the Virginia Company permission to colonize Bermuda, now known as Somers Isles. Colonialists establish town of St. George.

1614 The Virginia Company decides that Bermuda is a poor investment and surrenders the islands to the English Crown.

1615 King of England grants the Somers Islands Company a charter, but Bermuda remains subject to the Crown.

1617 The first mention of slaves in Bermuda appears in the record.

1620 The first General Assembly (Parliament) convenes in St. Peter's Church, St. George.

1668 Bermudians sail south and develop the salt industry in the Turks Islands.

1684 Bermuda reverts from a colony of the Somers Islands Company to direct rule by the British crown.

1775 Bermudians steal gunpowder from the armory in St. George and ship it to rebels in British colonies in America.

1812 Bermuda suffers the negative economic effects of the American-British war.

1815 Hamilton replaces St. George as Bermuda's capital.

1834 England abolishes slavery in Bermuda.

1846 Bermuda builds its first lighthouse, Gibbs Hill lighthouse, to end the practice of "wrecking" (looting) vessels stranded on reefs.

1861	The American Civil War starts and Bermudian vessels run the North's blockade to supply the Confederates.
1883	The daughter of Queen Victoria, Her Royal Highness Princess Louise, pays an official visit. The visit marks the rise of tourism in the islands.
1910	Bermuda declares motor vehicles illegal.
1923	Development of the Mid Ocean Club and Castle Harbour Hotel begins.
1930	United States passes tariff laws on agricultural produce, which severely damages Bermuda's agricultural-based economy.
1940	Due to the Second World War, American and British military personnel occupy Bermuda's main tourist hotels.
1946	Bermuda repeals the law banning motorcars, despite strong resistance from islanders.
1955	Dr. E.F. Gordon, a Member of Parliament and civil rights activist, dies.
1963	The Progressive Labor Party (PLP) is founded.
1965	The United Bermuda Party (UBP) is founded.
1968	Bermuda holds the first General Election under its new Constitution.
1973	Assassins kill Governor Sir Richard Sharples and four others.
1987	Hurricane Emily slams into the island, injuring many and causing millions of dollars in damage.
1995	A political referendum for independence fails. The American and British military bases close.
1998	PLP wins the general election for the first time. Bermudians make political history, as they elect Jennifer Smith as Premier, the first black woman to win a general election and to lead the government.
2003	PLP wins the general election for second straight time. The more moderate Alex Scott replaces Jennifer Smith as premier and PLP party leader in a leadership challenge. Bermuda becomes an associate (non-voting) member of the Caribbean Community (CARICOM).

CARICOM: Caribbean Community, an organization for the advancement of trade and economic development in the Caribbean region.

Commonwealth: The colonies and countries of the former British Empire that makeup the (British) Commonwealth for purposes of mutual security and assistance: the British Monarch as the symbolic head of this association.

Cash crop: A crop grown by a farmer primarily for sale to others rather than for his or her own use.

Colony: A territory that is distant from a country having control over it.

Condominium: An owner-occupied apartment that is in a large building or group of buildings.

Cricket: A popular British sport played with a leather ball and flat wooden bat by two teams with eleven players each on a large field. Teams compete by scoring runs.

Cruise ship: A ship used to carry a large group of tourists to one or more ports on a designated route.

Cuisine: French word for food.

Exports: Goods carried to other countries for the purposes of sale.

GDP: Gross Domestic Product, which is the value of all goods and services produced by a country.

Global economy: This term refers to the worldwide exchange of goods and services.

Good Friday: The Friday before Easter Sunday.

Great Britain: This is the principal island of the United Kingdom, including England, Scotland, and Wales.

Groundwater: Water found underground in porous rock strata and soils.

Hedgerow: A row of shrubs or bushes forming a boundary or fence called a hedge.

Imports: Goods brought from other countries to sell.

Limestone: A sedimentary rock composed of remains of sea animals, which is mainly hardened calcium carbonate (lime).

Mulatto: This is a person with a mixed black and white (Caucasian) ancestry.

Nature preserve: Natural territory set off limits to human habitation for the purpose of preserving endemic and native plants and animals.

Parish: This is a district of British local civil government.

PLP: Progressive Labor Party

Glossary

Privateering: This is a type of business venture: the sinking, harassing, or capturing of enemy ships for payment from a country.

Quarry: A place where building stone is dug up from the ground.

Rugby: This is English football. Two opposing teams play it. Players pass, kick or carry an oval ball toward a goal line. It is a forerunner of American football.

Salt works: A place where people mine salt.

Social club: An association of people who pay dues to be members. Members elect officers. Clubs' goals are usually to carry out charitable and recreational as well as social activities.

Smuggling: The secret transport of a good into or out of a country to avoid paying import or export taxes, respectively.

UBP: United Bermuda Party

United Kingdom: England, Wales, Scotland, Northern Ireland, and outer islands.

War on terrorism: The United States declared this "unofficial" war against all terrorist organizations and countries that harbor terrorists on September 11, 2001.

West Indies: Islands in the North Atlantic between North America and South America.

Wrecking: Bermudians use this term to describe looting of ships that have wrecked on reefs.

Ahiakpor, James C. W. *The economic aspects of political independence: the case of Bermuda.* Vancouver, B.C., Canada: Fraser Institute, 1990.

Bendure, Glenda, and Ned Friary. *Bermuda.* Hawthorne, Victoria, Australia: Lonely Planet Publications, 2000.

Bermuda Online. Economy of Bermuda depends on international business and tourism. *[http://bermuda-online.org/economy.htm]* accessed on November 15, 2004.

Bermuda Government Land Valuation Department *[http://www.agri.ns.ca/landval_lv/default.htm]* accessed November 13, 2004.

Bernhard, Virginia. *Slaves and Slaveholders in Bermuda 1616-1782.* Columbia, MO: University of Missouri Press, 1999.

Central Intelligence Agency. *The World Fact Book 2001.* Washington, D.C.: The U.S. Government Office, Superintendent of Documents, 2001.

Hannau, Hans W., rev. by William Zuill. *Bermuda in Full Color.* London: Macmillan Press Ltd, 1994.

Manning, Frank E. *Black Clubs in Bermuda: Ethnography of a Play World.* Ithaca, NY: Cornell University Press, 1973.

Regan, Nigel. "Bermuda must forge strategic alliances," *Bermuda Sun,* November 9, 2001.

Wilkinson, Henry Campbell. Bermuda from sail to steam: the history of the island from 1784 to 1901 (2 vols.). London: Oxford University Press, 1973.

World Gazetteer. Bermuda 2001. *[http://www.gazetteer.de/r/r_bm.htm]* accessed on November 15, 2004.

Zuill, W.S. *The Story of Bermuda and Her People,* 3rd ed. London: Macmillan Education Ltd, 1999.

Index

Picture Credits

DR. RICHARD A. CROOKER is a geography professor at Kutztown University in Pennsylvania, where he teaches physical geography, oceanography, map reading, and climatology. He received a Ph.D. in Geography from the University of California, Riverside. Dr. Crooker is a member of the Association of American Geographers and the National Council for Geographic Education. He has received numerous research grants, including three from the National Geographical Society. His publications deal with a wide range of geographical topics. He enjoys reading, hiking, bicycling, kayaking, and boogie boarding.

CHARLES F. ("FRITZ") GRITZNER is Distinguished Professor of Geography at South Dakota University in Brookings. He is now in his fifth decade of college teaching and research. During his career, he has taught more than 60 different courses, spanning the fields of physical, cultural, and regional geography. In addition to his teaching, he enjoys writing, working with teachers, and sharing his love for geography with students. As consulting editor for the MODERN WORLD NATIONS series, he has a wonderful opportunity to combine each of these "hobbies." Fritz has served as both President and Executive Director of the National Council for Geographic Education and has received the Council's highest honor, the George J. Miller Award for Distinguished Service. In March 2004, he won the Distinguished Teaching award from the American Association of Geographers at their annual meeting held in Philadelphia.